CW01500607

Acknowledgements

So many people have contributed to this publication, some taking weeks and months to read and re-read autobiographical accounts, compare notes, exchange theories and relentlessly study case files with me.

Many thanks to the kindest, most generous friends anyone could ever wish for. They have often held my hand through all of this and without their saintly patience, continued encouragement and sage advice this publication wouldn't have been possible. This counts for my mentor Kevin M. Sullivan in particular.

I also thank Kathleen Littell, Shirl Sipperley DiGugno, Gina Marzano Wilmoth, Sabrina Holmes, Eden O'Brien, Angela Abramovitz, Elissa Kerrill, Joanne Moss, Alexandra Kun, Alexandria Rose, Christina Murphy & Aaron Pyman, Jeff Canning, Annika Kaufert, Candace Caspers, C. Cortez, Mimi Kotner, Judi McCaffrey, Chris Morgan, Joe Ulam, EJ Hammon, Linda Graham, Cyndi Dean, Kelly Madison, Dr. Z, Dino Giampietro, Amber Berry, Emma Louise Brooks, Essa Zahir, Zach Hayes and eternally…the Passenger, as well as many kind strangers and acquaintances. Thank you to Abigail Hansmeyer and Meegan Senecal, who helped edit a few chapters, and to Katie Marcrum especially, who almost broke an arm (or possibly her neck) during the VW experiment she conducted for me.
I profusely apologize if I forgot to mention anyone by name.

I wish to thank my late father, one of the most resilient, humble and kind souls to have ever graced this earth, and my wonderful warrior queen of a mother for her enthusiasm in entertaining my various Bundy theories, going as far as attempting to recreate some of the unconfirmed survivor stories with me.

I must also thank Drew Bales. He first shared his impressions of some of these unconfirmed survivor stories with me and proposed the idea of examining them together in detail, encouraging me to first publish my observations on my *CrimePiper* blog.

I owe equal gratitude towards those who have been continually challenging me; our professional and personal disagreements continue to serve as inspiration to apply more patience and compassion in my daily life.

TED BUNDY
Examining The Unconfirmed Survivor Stories

by

ERIN BANKS

Disclaimer

Any opinions, statements of fact or fiction, descriptions, dialogue, and citations found in this book were provided by the author, and are solely those of the author.

Copyright 2021 by Erin Banks
1st edition, March 7, 2021

All rights reserved. No part of this book may be reproduced in any form or by any means without the prior written consent of the author, excepting brief quotes used in reviews.

Cover design 2020 by Erin Banks with Edit Org, https://edit.org
Interior Formatting by Erin Banks.

Index

Preface

Why this publication? Because of, and for:

Karen Sparks Epley. Carol DaRonch. Kathy Kleiner. Karen Chandler Pryor. Cheryl Thomas. – The confirmed survivors of Ted Bundy's brutality.

Equally, Leslie Parmenter. Kathleen Clara D'Olivo. Jane Curtis. Lorraine Fargo. Phyllis Armstrong. – Those who were unfortunate enough to have met Ted Bundy, yet fortunate enough to elude him.

And naturally, Lynda Ann Healy. Donna Gail Manson. Susan Rancourt. Roberta Kathleen Parks. Brenda Carol Ball. Georgann Hawkins. Janice Ann Ott. Denise Marie Naslund. Nancy Wilcox. Laura Ann Aime. Melissa Smith. Debra Jean Kent. Susan Curtis. Caryn Eileen Campbell. Julia Cunningham. Denise Oliverson. Lynnette Dawn Culver. Margaret Bowman. Lisa Levy. Kimberly Dianne Leach. As well as all unidentified and undiscovered victims.

Also, the Bundy family. The Boone family. The Kloepfers aka Kendalls. All victims' families and friends. All who were victimized by Ted Bundy in some way or another, due to his lies, his deceit, his manipulation, his theft, emotional, physical and sexual abuse.

Lastly, every single law enforcement officer, agent and psychologist who spent years working to bring justice to the victims and their families to the point of irrevocably impacting their physical and mental health.

There may be many more survivors whom we have not yet heard of, may never hear from, in part because it is possible they remain unaware how close they came to being murdered. – I am for instance reminded of the young woman bestselling author Kevin M. Sullivan wrote about in his second Bundy book, "*The Trail of Ted Bundy: Digging up the untold Stories.*" On the night of June 11, shortly before abducting Georgann Hawkins, Bundy had been spotted walking along Greek Row by co-ed Steve Burnham. He had deliberated offering the man on crutches, and visibly struggling with his briefcase, his help. But another young woman was quicker. Burnham watched her disappear into the darkness with Ted Bundy, and yet, we know that she survived because she re-emerged, walked back from carrying the briefcase to his vehicle unharmed.

Now, there have been other women to come forth in recent years who claimed to have survived Ted Bundy. In the majority of cases, they did not report these crimes perpetrated on them to the proper authorities. They waited up to several decades to speak up and instead of contacting law enforcement agencies they chose to contact the news media or publish their putative encounters in memoirs. Some are of the opinion that they chose attention or fame over their civic duty.

Unfortunately, this means that there is no substantial evidence that would confirm their stories, all evidence was either destroyed or corrupted, if indeed it existed.

However, there is also no concrete evidence to the contrary, yet it certainly is of interest to the Bundy community to examine these stories critically, with logic and reason, weighing their statements against known facts; all that which we know to be true beyond the shadow of a doubt about the serial killer, including his modus operandi and the timeline of events as thoroughly recorded by law enforcement.

Where were these women when their descriptions of Bundy and his VW would have aided law enforcement in apprehending him so much faster? None of them seem particularly bothered by possibly contributing to Bundy having had more victims than would have been necessary. Where were they in all these years when Bundy was but a fringe interest and the community transparent, small in numbers, and there were no annual book publications, new documentaries, movies with Hollywood beaus portraying Bundy as a heartthrob?

I sought to explore these questions, and many more, and set out to do so being completely neutral about their cases, particularly as I was still relatively new in the Bundy community when I first heard the names and stories of these women.

I had neither the preconceived notion to want to debunk them, nor to confirm them. But one thing has become painfully clear: While some, if not all, of these victims may have suffered through a violent event in their lives, I cannot say in good conscience that Bundy is a realistic suspect for several of them.

Which brings us to the final, the most crucial question: Why? Why may they have fabricated their stories, elements of their stories or cast blame on a high profile offender such as Bundy?

I will attempt to answer this question as best I can by detailing a few more prominently known cases in this publication.

Friends have repeatedly asked me whether I was sure I wanted to publish at all, as the subject matter was even more controversial than I apparently am. They feared it would be a metaphorical death sentence for me in a climate in which a mere allegation is enough for the public to determine the accused is guilty, and in which those who ask questions are considered accomplices.

One thing I have never been is a coward concerned with a bad reputation and equally bad Kindle or Goodreads ratings. The question is not whether I want to publish, rather, it's a necessity for me to do so because an allegation of any kind may never be enough but must be rigorously investigated. These women and men chose to publicly divulge their stories to us and keep retelling them in various formats. We who have written about them on our blogs or in our groups are not the ones who dragged them into the spotlight. We merely adjust that spotlight and shine it into corners of their stories that previously remained in the dark. Sometimes humor is necessary to point out precisely how unlikely certain components of the story are. This humor is not meant to defame, ridicule or harm the alleged survivors however.

This publication is my way – limited as it indisputably is – to contribute to a correction of course as it pertains to how we approach the unconfirmed survivor stories. And it is my sincerest hope that it may help end the incessant mythologizing of Ted Bundy.

March, 2021

Rhonda Stapley's Story

In 2016, Utah native Rhonda Godding, née Stapley, who spent portions of her childhood in Connell/Washington, published her autobiography "*I Survived Ted Bundy: The Attack, Escape & PTSD That Changed My Life.*" Her publication divides the Bundy community in equal parts to this very day.

Let me expound the most imperative thing first. It is as unwarranted as it is appalling to engage in ad hominem attacks towards Mrs. Stapley, or any unconfirmed survivor. I am confounded and dismayed to have witnessed known fixtures in the Bundy community resort to describe Stapley as too unattractive for Bundy to have raped her. I vehemently stand against this type of humiliation, and strongly believe that it does not reflect well on austere researchers standing idly by without demanding a certain conversational standard to be upheld in debates about unproven victims.

Mrs. Stapley's worth as a human being is indisputable. Her story is not. After careful analysis, I personally cannot consider Bundy to be a credible suspect for this crime, and a substantial amount of these conclusions I and other Bundy students came to, are based on more than mere circumstantial evidence.

In summer of 2018, hobby *YouTuber* Chris Mortensen, who occasionally dabbles in True Crime, provided Washington researcher Drew Bales and myself with a video he had taken while driving the route Ted Bundy supposedly took with Stapley on October 11, 1974. The drive took around an hour.

Provided with this general time frame, the following came to mind: Prior to her Bundy encounter, the young lady had had dental surgery, her mouth and jaw were sore, she was overall miserable. Is it then plausible that she would go on an extended drive with a stranger, simply because she thought him charming and handsome, but predominantly because she did not want to embarrass him by asking him to please not take a detour? Or because she was under the impression that his intention was to make out with her?

Even if Bundy had been so inclined to want to kiss a woman with a swollen mouth, cheek and bleeding gums, that she would have been eager to let him is more difficult to believe.

One need only think back to one's own experience with dental surgery; the duration of not being able to speak, drink, eat, swallow – let alone kiss - without great pain and difficulty is substantial. I posit that romance is conventionally the last thing on one's mind under those circumstances.

Now granted, this is mere circumstantial evidence at best, yet these questions are not unfair to pose.

Stapley claims Bundy took her to a public spot with a picnic table. We are asked to accept that a skilled murder rapist like Bundy attacked the woman in broad daylight, starting at approximately 3.00 to 3.30 P.M., where anyone could have driven by or stopped for a picnic. The latter is not a far-fetched thought, as Stapley affirms that it was an unusually warm and sunny day for October. This may have been the last chance for Utahns to bask in the sunlight before months of snow and an average temperature of 37°F. With the campus in relative proximity, it appears likely that on this particular Friday afternoon people would have been bustling about everywhere, especially anywhere around a picnic table.

Bundy's modus operandi is well known; his confessions matched the discoveries and informed assumptions of investigators; he chose secluded spots to rape and kill. He was meticulous and alert in Washington, Oregon, Utah, Idaho and Colorado, availing himself of his wide knowledge of the law, and law enforcement procedures.

In Utah, Bundy was not in the state of psychosis he was in while in Florida. There his approach was sloppy, and the kill compulsion prompted him to attempt the daytime kidnapping of 14-year old Leslie Parmenter and 12-year old Kimberly Leach in the middle of the street.

Stapley further purports the myth of the "broken door handle." However, the 1968 VW Beetle would not open if the outside door handle was still attached to the door while the inner door handle had been dismounted. Several researchers have credibly demonstrated this in the past.

If the inner latch had been dismounted, the integral part of the door handle - the cylinder/pin, latch assembly and mounting screws holding inside and outside of the door handles together, and only separated by the door/panel itself - would sit loosely in the door. If one now tugged on the outer latch in an attempt to open the door, one would inevitably pull out the entire door handle from the outside.

Readers who remain in doubt may wish to try this with any regular door in their homes without fearing to do irreparable damage, and the result will be the same.

Imagine driving around the rocky roads of Utah with a loose door handle in place. Motion, speed bumps, potholes. Does it sound likely the door handle would not come off at some point during a drive through partly uneven territory?

Moreover, the door handle story makes no sense whatsoever when poring over the schematics of the car, and VW confirmed this to me as well upon my contacting them.

Considering the time it would have taken to keep dismounting and remounting the door handle each time Bundy went on the prowl for suitable victims, why go through the trouble at all? We know Bundy used handcuffs (and other binding material like rope and cords) because he was a methodical control freak with many obsessive-compulsive traits as it pertains to his M.O., but most of all he was a minimum effort type of person. Less elegantly put, he was incredibly lazy, not just as a student, but as a killer as well. Handcuffs did the trick, and he always had them on hand.

Skeptics unconvinced that the door handle remained in its rightful place at all times during Bundy's murderous activities, pondered whether Bundy may have glued the outer door handle on in order to render the door operable despite the inner door handle missing. Though such mental gymnastics irritate me to no end, let's entertain this theory for a moment. We must ask ourselves whether Bundy first unglued the door handle each time he attacked a woman, only to have to glue it back on after the crime's completion, so as not to rouse Kloepfer's suspicion? This seems like a stretch and might have damaged the mechanism or at least the paint which no one ever reported on.

And we must remember that when DaRonch escaped Bundy, the door handle was where it always had been. She opened the car from inside without trouble when she escaped, handcuffs still dangling from her wrist. The same handcuffs Bundy mentioned so many times throughout his confessions to Robert Keppel, Dennis Couch, Bill Hagmaier and others.

We must then inquire why Bundy would reattach the door handle in November for the DaRonch and Debra Jean Kent abductions after it had been missing, and proven effective, for his October kidnapping of Stapley. The door handle myth – unnecessarily and unfathomably - has become the Ouroboros question of Bundy researchers.

Returning to questions regarding his modus operandi, why would Bundy strike all confirmed victims over the head with a crowbar, but not any of the unconfirmed victims, including Stapley? Even before he had graduated to being a serial killer, Bundy had always immediately rendered the victim unconscious so as to prevent them from escaping.

Even when committing his first amateurish 1972 attacks on women out on the street he had used blunt objects, such as discarded wood, to target his victims' heads as soon as he had gained access to them.

Stapley further states that Bundy played perverse asphyxiation games with her, strangling and reviving her multiple times over the course of multiple hours. That he was capable of such a heinous act is nothing I would ever doubt, and he himself admitted to having strangled victims from behind with rope or cord. That Bundy perpetrated such an attack in the middle of the day in a public spot isn't plausible to me. There are further questions regarding the logistics of the attack which I will only mention in this sentence, and in passing, so as not to be distasteful. Astute readers will know what I'm referring to.

Bundy was so invested in his "Entity career" that he had put together a murder kit in order to always be prepared. He kept his kill tools, coveralls, trash bags and other needed items at the ready.
Would Bundy leave Stapley unsupervised to rummage around in his car with his back turned towards her, despite him being aware that she had reawakened after each asphyxiation? What was he rummaging around for in his vehicle? Anything he needed was in his kill kit.

Furthermore, Stapley claims she took a few stumbling steps at the edge of the river - still with her pants around her ankles – and fell right into the icy current which swept her away to safety. The river in question is surrounded by large rocks and boulders, visible on photos taken of the location, visible on videos I was provided with, and confirmed to me by a person living in the area.
It then follows that Stapley would have had to stumble across rocks and boulders in the dead of night, in a place without street lamps or other illumination, with her pants down, and without ever just falling or tripping once before ultimately landing in the river.
Another question that arises is the state of the river during fall, or more specifically October. People living in the area have confirmed to me that the river is but a mere puddle, just a few short inches high during fall and winter.

Stapley writes in her book that she later detected she had broken her ribs, and here is why many researchers have contested this claim:
After her final reawakening from asphyxiation, Stapley will have experienced an adrenaline rush. Adrenaline is produced in the adrenal glands above the kidneys, and its

effects include numbing the body from feeling physical pain, sharpening the mental focus while under threat, and increasing physical strength for a limited amount of time. It's likely that Stapley initially didn't feel any pain, was hence not immobilized yet - as one typically is when breaking one's ribs.

However, she walked 14 miles back to her dorm room. The average female person with her assumed level of fitness due to her age, height (4'11), weight and lifestyle, walks a mile within 15-20 minutes. We must also consider the fact she would have been injured and had difficulty walking due to the physical rape trauma, as well as the strangulation, which would have made it hard to breathe, keeping her from walking at all too briskly a pace.

Add to this that she experienced pain in her jaw due to dental surgery and because Bundy, she states, also raped her orally, ripping out the stitching in her cheek in the process. This pain would have been severe and added to problems swallowing and breathing while trekking home. She may very well have had to stop on occasion to catch her breath.

All of this points to her having taken much longer to walk these 14 miles. If we consider for a moment, that one mile may have taken her 25-30 minutes to walk, this accounts for a time frame of at least six hours.

The attack on her occurred, as mentioned earlier, around 3-3.30 P.M. It was dark when she awoke, which means it must have been after 7 P.M. – the time of sunset in Salt Lake City on October 11, 1974.

Despite the aforementioned issue of the low water level, we do not know how much time Stapley may have spent in the river. I estimate that it should not have been longer than fifteen minutes as her body temperature would have dropped so dangerously low that her chances of survival would have been slim. She would at least have developed pneumonia, especially after walking in the cold Utah night for several hours at a stretch while soaking wet.

Stapley does not mention being dripping wet. No one who saw her that night came running to inquire about the state she was in or whether she required medical attention. This strikes me as unusual for that era and time of night, particularly in a Mormon college town.

Two more compelling details were provided by an acquainted psychotherapist in training who has worked in the field of emergency services. Within that context, Emma Louise Brooks had closely worked with a water rescue instructor who answered several

13

of her questions regarding the chance of survival in an icy current while fully clothed and with one's pants bunched around the ankles.

The instructor recommended precisely what I also gathered from numerous websites, among them *"The Active Times."* In their article, *"How To Survive A Fast River Current,"* it is written,

"The method experts recommend most is going down on your back, with your feet pointed downstream, and your head positioned upstream. This way, your head is protected and your legs will take any of the damage from rocks and debris. The top half of your feet should be poking out of the water and your head should be above water as well. Look downstream and keep calm, breathe with the flow of the water, to keep from swallowing too much water. When you come up on a calmer area, flip over and swim diagonally toward shore, with the flow of the current."

Alternatively, the author of the article presents a second, albeit less popular method, suggesting to swim on one's stomach, head-first downstream as it is easier to control one's direction in this position. However, they caution the reader that one's head would be more vulnerable to impact with rocks and branches.

According to experts, survival chances are low if one attempts to swim, paddle or does not assume the correct posture – stiff as a board - in a river current, its ripples pulling a person underwater where one will swiftly lose sight of the surface.

On page 37 of her autobiography Stapley writes,

"I flailed about, struggling for breath, in the freezing water, but when I opened my mouth, I swallowed gulps of cold river. I choked, fighting for my life, as my body was smashed against rocks."

That Stapley would have survived her inexpert battle with the river current is astounding enough. That she repeatedly connected with rocks and debris without breaking another bone, and even survived floating in the river while unconscious, is truly miraculous.

The above mentioned emergency-trained researcher further reported that she had contacted a physician at a local, UK-based hospital in order to learn more about the physical trauma strangulation conventionally causes.

Based on the doctor's assessment, she relayed to me,

"Given that Stapley was repeatedly manually strangled, significant hemorrhaging would have occurred inside and around the eyes and area of the mouth, and she would have had visible edemas around her neck, resulting in cartilage damage in the trachea and larynx. Loss of oxygen to the brain might have disabled the victim to the point of being unable to walk or be able to properly move," even despite above mentioned adrenaline rush. *"There would have long term vocal damage if the injuries were untreated, which could have been life-threatening."*

It is equally peculiar that Bundy would not have driven up and down along the river to look for Stapley. She had seen him up close for numerous hours, could hence provide sketch artists with a decent description of him and his vehicle and its interior. She knew where and what he studied, and most imperatively, she could even have provided law enforcement with his first name. How long would it have taken for law enforcement to identify a young UU law student named Ted who drove a VW Beetle? An hour perhaps?

The author comforts herself with the notion that her ID only showed her previous address, rendering her safe from further harm by Bundy. A strange notion, considering he could have found her due to the fact she had divulged to him what she was studying. Bundy, an expert level stalker, may have lurked about the building and lecture hall. He could have easily followed her to find out her current address and attacked whenever she was home alone, or better yet, while she was out on her nightly runs after the assault.

The most baffling part of Stapley's above statement is yet that she felt no urge to warn residents at both her old and new address that a murder-rapist might possibly come looking for her? Another question: Did the new tenants know her new address? Wasn't she worried they might provide Bundy with it? Or that he may have harmed anyone else living at her previous address to elicit information from them about her current whereabouts?

That she showed no regard for her own life is tragic, albeit her own choice. That she showed none for anyone else's life is maddening.

Stapley is of the mind that her mother would have taken her out of school had she learned of the attack on her daughter. That seems illogical because we know that Stapley was relatively close to graduating and her family was in dire need of the money after her father's passing. While these are more "cold and calculated" reasons, let me offer an emotional component for deliberation. I have trouble believing that her mother would not have felt the urge to rush to her child's aid, doing anything and everything to keep her safe, including convincing her daughter to report the attack to the campus and the authorities.

Had she done so, Carol DaRonch, Debbie Kent, Caryn Campbell, Julie Cunningham, Denise Oliverson, and perhaps even Kimberly Leach, Margaret Bowman, Lisa Levy, Kathy Kleiner, Karen Chandler and Cheryl Thomas could have been spared. He would have been arrested before his Colorado murders and not extradited to the state that let him escape not once but twice, sharing at least a part of the blame for the Florida crimes. Instead Stapley strongly implies that her boots are secretly to blame for her not contacting police.

"…because when I crawled out of the river I would have been barefoot and probably naked and unable to just walk home and pretend nothing had happened. Without that sturdy footwear I could not have managed the long trek home. Someone would certainly have known what had happened to me if not for those high-topped, double-knotted boots."

The bottom line is that had Stapley arrived at a police station in her disheveled state, there isn't one police officer in the world who would have questioned that she experienced a traumatic event. There would have been plenty of physical evidence to corroborate it.

So her allegation that police might have not believed her because women were habitually doubted when reporting a rape or violent crime of any kind during this era, rings false. We know for a fact police did not doubt DaRonch, who arrived at the station quivering, in a state of shock, and with cuffs on her wrist. DaRonch was questioned on the exact circumstances of the event, what the offender had looked like, what he wore, what state he was in, what car he drove, whether she had seen him before. These questions neither denote disbelief nor an attack on her; they are necessary to ask for police to put together a case. DaRonch was further questioned on the stand, and Dr. Elizabeth Loftus – to whom I have dedicated a short chapter at the end of this publication – cast some doubt on aspects she remembered that were later shown not to have occurred the way they did. Not even that is an attack on DaRonch or any other survivor. There is no emotion involved in investigating a crime, only facts matter. DaRonch remained firm in her assertions, and all other substantial evidence helped convict Bundy. Without question, it would have gone the same way for Rhonda Stapley.

Stapley mentions shame as a driving factor in her not reporting the rape. We'll need to dig a little into the religion of Latter Day Saints in order to understand how sexual assault is officially – and actually – viewed by the church.

From the *Book Of Mormon*:

"For behold, many of the daughters of the Lamanites have they taken prisoners; and after depriving them of that which was most dear and precious above all things, which is chastity and virtue…"

Having spent many months with the LDS in the past, it is not solely because of the above paragraph that I can state with certainty that what is indeed most precious to Latter Day Saints to be virtuous, which encompasses chastity.
To lose one's virginity out of wedlock and/or due to rape irrevocably annihilates it. Rape survivors have laden upon them sin, shame, they are without virtue, unclean, "less than." Far be it from me to criticize anyone's religious delusions, yet this particular passage is abhorrently abusive and incorrect, plain and simple.
Furthermore, victims may be held responsible for having been raped, the Law Of Chastity of the Mormon church officially states this is not so, but Mormon "Apostle" Richard G. Scott made clear that,

"The victim must do all in his or her power to stop the abuse. [...] At some point in time, however, the Lord may prompt a victim to recognize a degree of responsibility for abuse. [...]"

Victims of sexual assault have been known to react with paralysis, with overt aggression, with tears, with hysteric laughter, with dissociation and silence. All of these reactions are deemed sinful apparently. This is what actual victim-shaming looks like. If I knew my fellow believers considered me "sullied in the eyes of God," I would also have been deeply ashamed of having been attacked.
So while I empathize with this aspect of the Stapley case, and fully acknowledge that shame may have played a large part in Stapley not wanting to reveal the attack to family, friends and her church, I must yet remain firm in my conclusion that no matter one's religiosity, the mere thought of being able to prevent such a crime to happen to anyone else would always, ALWAYS, take precedence. There is no acceptable explanation or excuse for Stapley not having reported Bundy to the authorities.

After Stapley finally returned home, she assessed her injuries. She had a goose egg over her eye, was badly bruised and beaten, her ribs hurt. Her roommates – intellectually astute academics – believed her assertion that the goose egg and facial bruising were scars contracted in the course of dental surgery.

She went about her daily routine as per usual within the following days and weeks to come, so her ribs cannot possibly have been broken. After my mother broke two ribs in 2020, I was forced to move in with her to care for her day and night. She could hardly breathe, she could neither dress nor bathe herself and was incapable of lifting up her elbows more than two inches without bursting into tears.

It's remarkable that Stapley, a pharmacology student with basic medical knowledge, ignored the danger of not having her midsection x-rayed to determine which and how many ribs were fractured, as well as what type of fractures she was looking at. Broken ribs require immediate treatment, pain medication and constant attention. Without this, and without rest, she could have easily punctured a lung and was at risk of her ribs fusing back incorrectly. That a pharmacology student would take such a risk is grotesque.

Stapley reports in her book that when she was finally ready to date again, she left little notes for her roommates underneath the garbage bag in the apartment's trashcan, in case her date decided to murder her. This is curious for two reasons. First of all, why did she place the notes underneath the garbage bag if she wanted them found? What about leakage that could have easily rendered the note unreadable? What if the note had gotten stuck on the garbage bag due to leakage? In that case it would have been tossed in the dumpster never to be seen again.

Why not just tell one of her roommates she was going out on a date with person X? No cloak and dagger business needed. No one would have suspected she was once raped just because she was being responsible by sharing some basic details about her upcoming date with someone whom law enforcement would question after her disappearance. In fact, every single of my female friends and family members alerts at least one person prior to going on a date, or if they buy something off of Craigslist, for that matter.

Stapley, however, is of the opinion that it was enough that someone would "at some point" find her note to solve the case of her murder. Well, I don't know, but would it not be logical to want roommates or law enforcement to find this note as soon as possible and immediately after a possible abduction, in case she is still alive somewhere? This component of the story certainly adds suspense, even an oddly dark romanticism perhaps, but it is lacking in credibility in my view.

While reading her memoir, I was increasingly left with the impression that Stapley was rather fond of attention, most of all attention afforded to her by powerful men. Dr. Victor Cline, whom Stapley *"knew in passing"* from church, was a *"well-known psychologist, [...] professor and [...] assistant dean in the Psychology Department at the University of Utah,"* and the first man to take a personal interest in her after the attack. He was reportedly assigned to be her new home teacher. The LDS church assigns home teachers to all members of a household. But in Stapley's case, he was assigned to her alone. Cline allegedly boasted that he was famous, and that people paid a lot of money for private counseling sessions from him, but here he was, offering them to her for free. He even arranged for her to study in the faculty lounge, without any academic achievement on her part. It's significant to mention that Cline was not aware of the attack perpetrated on Stapley at the time. She believes he – a virtual stranger – just "seemed to sense" that something was wrong with her. To take such an extensive and personal interest in a female student, considering the obvious possible connotations of the nature of his interest, is astounding for someone with as much to lose as Cline did. It's "not recommended" by the LDS that a man and woman who are not married or not otherwise related to one another interact without witnesses present or in great frequency.

Still, according to Stapley, Cline continued showering young Rhonda with attention. He helped her drop a class she was failing, and he facilitated this in the most offensive manner possible. *"Watch this,"* he had allegedly smirked as he picked up the phone. Instead of asking his colleague, he informed him that Stapley *would* not return to his class and was not to be failed for it either. Cline, despite his standing, wasn't afraid of repercussions from his colleagues or the university. He put his employment on the line for a random girl because she "seemed sad."

On one occasion, Cline informed Stapley that he was to give a lecture that students were not permitted to attend. But he wanted her to come, yes, he needed her kind face to look back up at him while lecturing. If he required a kind face, why did he not ask his wife or children to tag along?

This storyline repeats itself twice more in the book, at least in principle, as it involves not Cline but other "characters."

For one, there is Stapley's quasi-suicide attempt during which she calls a crisis hotline and the person on the other end, Dave, then swoops in to save the day by turning up on her doorstep.

It is significant to note that staff and volunteers at DEM/DES in Washington and Utah confirmed to me that call responders are trained to never leave their post under any circumstances in order to go to a caller's house. They would be terminated effective immediately if they were to visit a caller after completion of their shift.

Instead, call takers are required to call the proper authorities if they fear that someone is in danger of harming themselves or others, all the while keeping the caller on the line to stall/assess the situation/calm them down.

Even True Crime writer Ann Rule, who worked at a crisis hotline with Ted Bundy in 1972, confirms this protocol in her book, *The Stranger Beside Me*.

I will not delve too deeply into Stapley's prescription drug abuse and dependence, although it's worrisome that after a customer had taken back his bottle of Placydil to the drugstore, Stapley's superior supposedly told her to just keep it rather than follow protocol by safely disposing of it. Well. It was the 70's, I surmise.

What I'm far more interested in is how she kept acquiring Placydil. Nowhere in her memoir does she mention that a general practitioner prescribed it to her. We must consider that she may have acquired it illegally, and that the drug abuse may have also done its part to alter her perception or even part of her memory.

Decades later, Stapley and previous crisis hotline volunteer Dave – now Dr. David – meet again.

That Dr. David believed Stapley was attacked by Ted Bundy we can of course not outright dismiss. He may have done so. A therapist's job is not to assess the credibility of a patient's story but to help them handle their emotions and change problematic thought patterns. In case the therapist becomes aware that he is dealing with a delusional person, he may attempt to slowly open up the patient's mind to the possibility of falsified memory or a generally distorted perception.

One example in which psychotherapists shared in an unfortunate mass delusion is the "Satanic Panic" of the 80's and 90's, which was sparked by the book *"Michelle Remembers"* by Michelle Smith. All too many psychologists and therapists were swept up in the hype, suspending critical thinking for conspiracy theories that were later completely debunked. I'm mentioning this because according to Stapley, her therapist went a tad further than to just believe she was attacked by Ted Bundy. He began researching Bundy and his case almost obsessively, spending many a private moment reading Bundy-related books and going as far as obtaining the offender's FBI files.

Perhaps the man covertly harbored the dream of becoming a Detective, who knows? It's not entirely out of the question, since he allegedly told Stapley that he had *"tried several other careers over the years,*" but being a therapist was what he always came back to. What is harder to swallow is Stapley's assertion that concluding his Bundy studies, the good doctor handed his patient his notes so she would see black in white that he admired her then, and he admired her now! This is followed by more gibberish, such as telling her that Stapley was his hero. In fact, Dr. David felt unworthy to be with her in the face of her courage and determination. He allegedly closed his impassionate appraisal of her flawless character with, "*I put you on a pedestal right alongside my family members who work as first responders or who have been in military combat.*" And, of course, if these were his last two hours on earth, he would have loved to have spent them listening to Stapley telling him all about her sexual assault. Forget his wife, his children, his entire family! Rhonda is where it's at. Nothing in the world can convince me that we're not being taken on a ride here.

Not only does Stapley make Dr. David sound like the most unethical therapist to have ever existed, but we must remember that David's outburst came after he had not seen Stapley in some forty years. Yet he had "greeted her like an old friend," admitting he had always wondered when she would seek him out. This isn't exactly a flattering statement to make if you think about it, by the way.

Another problem is that Stapley could not have anticipated that Dave would become a psychotherapist, so his alleged statement makes no sense. Likewise, we are asked to accept that a woman he'd met only once in his life – one of thousands of callers, thousands of people he'd worked with in the "unique" multitude of professions he'd worked in throughout his life – was so special that he developed an unhealthy and unprofessional desire to see her again. He "waited" for her. He is made to sound as though he were not a prince on a white stallion but a prince with a white straight jacket. All bitter irony aside, therapists are discouraged from using overly emotional or familial language when speaking to their clients so as not to cause Transference, which is detrimental to therapy and can result in severe mental and emotional disruptions for both client and mental health professional alike.

The ultimate jumping the shark moment occurs when Stapley claims that Bundy's bite mark re-appeared on her left breast nearly forty years after the attack. Physically re-appeared that is, a type of "True Crime stigmata." This is a surprisingly Catholic element to add for a Latter Day Saint. It is made absolutely certain the reader understand that this was an actual and real wound, swollen, hurting and bleeding, and that there was nothing metaphorical about it. I consulted three acquainted Latter Day Saints who confirmed to me that stigmata – be they True Crime-related or not – are not part of the LDS faith.

There were yet more stigmata to suffer for Rhonda Stapley. On one occasion as she was out driving her car, she suddenly remembered how sore her gums had been on the day of the Bundy attack. This memory, she writes, triggered her gums to literally bleed, then and there in her vehicle, decades later.

If nothing else I wrote convinced you that several components of Stapley's story are dubious, then this absolutely should.

What is perhaps most alarming Stapley strongly implies in her book that her husband Barry refuses to support her. The way she writes about him he remains but an ominous, Rumplestiltskin-esque villain throwing temper tantrums about his wife's quest to tell "her truth," and often insulting her with insensitive remarks about finally getting over that pesky rape all those years ago.

Still, I would have loved to hear his voice in her book. He could have added much to our understanding of Stapley's struggles, her emotional and mental state. And I equally would have welcomed his presence on the *Dr. Phil* show, on which Stapley recited her story in 2016. He could have helped educate the public about the challenges family and friends of those with a sexual assault trauma face.

In a 2016 status updates on one of her *Facebook* profiles, Stapley speaks of how relieved she is that her husband is finally recovering after his heart attack, for she can now finally get back to promoting and selling her book. I found this statement to be incredibly tone deaf and revealing as to her own level of empathy.

Stapley did not mention that she was glad Barry was recovering for his sake but because he had separated her from the adulation the general public showered her with while on her book signing tours.

I'll cement my claim with a quote from her autobiography:

"...Barry] seemed to think that I was dredging up ancienthistory for some devious purpose. I got the impression he thought that I wascompeting with him — that I had decided to become upset about a long agotrauma just as he was dealing with his own health crisis."

Stapley generally appears rather prone to "competing" with others. For one, she frequently points to her and her family's prestige in her memoir. Mentioning her father's fatal plane crash that occurred when she was a young teenager, she cannot do so without pointing to her family's nation-wide fame due to patenting several potato products, in other words potato recipes. *"Our family became sort of like celebrities," I said [to Dr. David]. Everyone knew who we were…"*

After her father's passing she chose the tie tack that had pierced his heart and lung as a keepsake. As if that were not enough in terms of uniqueness already, she appears unable of letting her late father have his own moment and proceeds to mention that she keeps the pin in question in a box with her own gallstones. *"…my gallstones are actually very pretty, almost like polished gemstones."*

Several years ago, I stumbled upon a *KATU-AM Northwest* interview on *YouTube* from June 22, 2016 in which Stapley was asked about Carol DaRonch's brave escape. At 7:55 minutes into the video, Stapley has the gall to conclude: *"She escaped as soon as she got into the car, so she wasn't really assaulted."* Regrettably, the interviewer did not press her further on this repulsive and outrageous statement. DaRonch was "not really assaulted." Meaning DaRonch isn't really a victim. Is that so? Let's review.

Bundy turns to slap the first handcuff on DaRonch's wrists. She panics. She struggles. Bundy tries to put the second handcuff on her. She fights back and he beats her, tries to subdue her. He cuffs her on the same wrist. DaRonch opens the car door. Pushes herself out with both legs, landing hard on the asphalt. Scrambles to her feet. Bundy pursues her, crowbar in hand. He strikes at the petite woman. She blocks his attack. He strikes again. And again. And again. Mrs. Stapley, this is precisely what assault looks like.

It is cruel to suggest that because the assault didn't last "longer," or because she wasn't sexually assaulted, DaRonch isn't a true survivor. To imply that she – who insisted Mary and Wilbur Walsh immediately drive her to the Murray police station despite the couple's initial rejection – isn't anything short of a heroine, an example of resilience and determination, is reprehensible.

What Stapley did in this interview is comparing pain. It's opening up a discussion for what constitutes having been harmed "enough" to deserve basic human empathy.

Without DaRonch, Bundy would have continued to kill far longer. Stapley could have contributed to that. She actively chose not to do so. In conclusion, Stapley didn't just need powerful men such as Dr. Cline and Dave/Dr. David to consider her special beyond comparison, but she goes as far as basking in her self-assumed special status even among survivors. Why can she not be a sister in survival, sharing the "limelight" with them? Are they seriously competitors to her?

It is somewhat frightening that Stapley reacts with a disproportional amount of aggression when merely asked questions regarding timeline, factual errors in her accounts – such as the myth of the missing door handle – or the logistics of her escape.

She went as far as threatening to sue a prominent Bundy author for simply stating that he found <u>some</u> of her statements questionable.

What also worries me is one particular photo of Stapley's in which she holds up an issue of *Real Crime* next to her face, beaming into the camera with frantic eyes. It's none other than Ted Bundy's visage depicted on the magazine cover.

The author posted this photo on her memoir's *Facebook* page, as well as on her two known *Facebook* accounts. Stapley's story was featured in this issue of *Real Crime*, but as a crime survivor myself, I struggle to find the words to articulate my discomfort that a woman would put her face next to that of her rapist, looking rather elated and proud. Some people reminded me that victims handle their feelings, their grief and outrage, in their own ways. That much is true, I can corroborate this from my own experiences. But I have yet to come across a rape survivor who actively seeks out to constantly connect her name and her face to a known serial rapist and killer such as Bundy. This strikes me as very unusual.

Moreover, Stapley has used both her autobiography and her *Facebook* pages to keep advertising her Snugglehose business. That is, of course, a very clever business strategy, if it's tasteful or appropriate is another matter entirely.

It is quite possible that Stapley was attacked by someone, I have no pressing reason to doubt it, in fact. If she was assaulted, then it is also almost guaranteed she suffered from PTSD and a myriad of other emotional or mental health issues, as many survivors do. However, I cannot in good conscience say that it is believable to me the perpetrator, "*my bad guy*," as she keeps affectionately referring to him as though he were a James Dean type rebel, was Ted Bundy.

Sotria Kritsonis' Story

In early 2018, a Washington State news agency, Kiro Channel 7, conducted an interview with a woman named Sotria Kritsonis. I watched the interview several times in order to understand the timeline of events and specific allegations contained therein. It was important for me to get a sense of the weather, and the time of year this presumed encounter transpired. Ultimately, these indications helped me determine whether Ted Bundy could be considered a suspect in this case. In my personal opinion he is not. Once more, this is not to say that Kritsonis may not have been attacked by someone other than Bundy. Although a few aspects of her story would still warrant further questioning in my view.

In her interview, Kritsonis immediately insists that Bundy's eyes were "dark." Bundy's face was reportedly shaded by the roof of his car, so his eyes may indeed have appeared dark to Kritsonis. However, I suspect the reason she mentions Bundy's eyes at all, is to offer indisputable "evidence" that the kidnapper could have been none other than Bundy. Which is undoubtedly based on the common narrative by many unconfirmed survivors, as well as interrogators and psychologists, that whenever his "Entity" overtook him, his eyes changed color.

I have extensively written about the phenomenon of *Mydriasis* in a previous article for *CrimePiper*, *"Ted Bundy: Metaphysical Myths & The Entity." Mydriasis* is the extreme dilation of the pupils due to an extreme emotional reaction. To the untrained eye it's easily mistaken for a supernatural phenomenon.

Yet Kritsonis' statement seems to cater directly to the metaphysical myths mob who prefer to speculate about demonic possession, rather than understand psychopathology or simple physiological reactions.

Kritsonis goes on to state that Bundy reached underneath his seat. — Here she breaks off, and the interviewer unfortunately doesn't inquire further as to what the purpose of Bundy doing so would have been. The first thing that came to mind to us who discussed the interview was Kritsonis meant to invoke the image of Bundy reaching for the crowbar, perhaps making sure it was in place for a later attack on her.

It is important to remember that Bundy, in true boy scout fashion, was "always prepared," as we know from his kills Washington, Utah and Colorado kills. This detail of Kritsonis' story is oddly reminiscent of Rhonda Stapley's account that Bundy went to dig around in his car as she awoke on the picnic table in the Utah canyon, giving her the chance to make her daring escape.

And yet another tidbit, that we have otherwise only ever found in Stapley's accounts, is that Kritsonis claims she was picked up at a bus stop – which was not a part of Bundy's modus operandi. In Washington, Bundy targeted women on campuses, in their homes, in bars, in Utah he targeted high schoolers that he snatched off the street or lured towards his car. He targeted females who were unaccompanied and usually did so after dark. The exception to the rule being the Lake Sammamish abductions, because he banked on the face-blindness of people in large crowds, and while under the influence of alcohol and other intoxicants.

According to Kritsonis, Bundy at once became aggressive with her. He inquired why she had climbed in the car with him in the first place, divulging to her that she ought not to have done that because in doing so she had forced his hand, he would have to kill her based on that fact alone.

This strange erratic outburst is more congruent with the behavior or deluded thinking of a visionary (psychotic) killer, not with Bundy and his ilk. We do not know how exactly Bundy interacted with each and every one of his victims, other than what he admitted to investigators, and what we learned from the confirmed survivors. We have to rely, in part, on textbooks such as the *"Crime Classification Manual"* to determine what a hedonistic and power/control killer conventionally acts like with his victims. Undoubtedly, our strongest eyewitness is Carol DaRonch, who escaped the killer after she had entered his car. Similarly to what Bundy confessed regarding his deceased victims, Bundy immediately attacked DaRonch, tried to cuff and strike her over the head with the crowbar.

There was no verbal interaction involved after she had entered his car, and why would it have? Bundy told FBI agent Bill Hagmaier that *"[the victims] can be anything you want them to be."* As soon as a woman entered his car, she lost her status as a human being and became a puppet instead. Someone he could fantasize into a preferred role. A conversation would have disrupted this fantasy.

The behavior Kritsonis mentions seems out of character for Bundy.

The door handle myth poses the biggest problem in Kritsonis' story. Particularly because of her claim that Bundy kicked her out of the car in front of her university. How would he have opened the door from the inside if the door handle was missing? This part of the story cannot be true.

Kritsonis does also not mention Bundy getting out of the car to open the door for her. Yet he couldn't have opened the car door for her from the inside if the door handle was missing.

Just as in Stapley's case, Kritsonis does not mention handcuffs, although Bundy attested to using them on almost all of his victims. Below is a photo of the infamous "Utah kill kit," taken by the late Detective Jerry Thompson. Note the handcuffs:

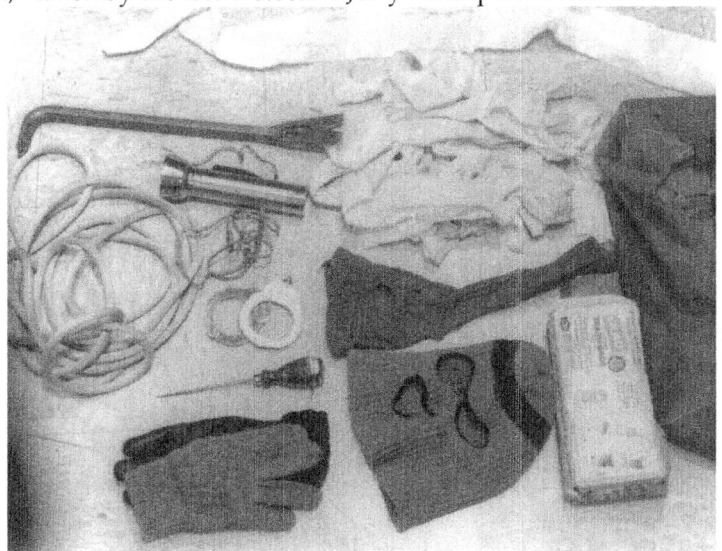

Photo: SLCSO and KCA

What would Bundy require handcuffs for if he dismounted the inner door handle to ensure a victim would not be able to escape? And the opposite holds true as well, why go through the trouble of dismounting the door handle if handcuffs were available to him? In fact, a missing door handle would have aroused the suspicion of any astute victim. The victims would have also been alerted of a missing door handle if Bundy's assistance was required to close the door from outside, in which case any victim would immediately raise hell to try to escape.

So no matter from which angle we tackle this issue, the door handle story simply does not pan out.

The next oddity in the story is the claim that Bundy let Kritsonis go because took offense to the length of her hair. I of course take into consideration the fact that Lisa Levy was not only a chance victim who was blitz attacked in her bed, but that it was dark in Levy's dorm room. Kill-frenzied Bundy in all likelihood didn't bother checking the length of her hair to determine if she was his "type." Type had little to do with the Chi

Omega Sorority attack.

Yet there were other victims whose hair was shorter, Campbell's, Rancourt's, Culver's and Leach's for example.

It is possible that Bundy may have preferred long hair, and it appears he did have an affinity for brunettes. However, smooth long hair parted in the middle was in style in the 70's, and brown is the dominant hair color in the USA, so it does not come as a surprise that more of his victims were brunettes with this particular hairdo.

Author Ann Rule's claim that Bundy killed solely dark haired girls with their long hair parted in the middle is untrue, as is clearly visible from the victim photographs available to the public. Their hair colors ranged from blonde, to various shades of brown and black.

That he would get hung up on the length of a victim's hair to the point of dismissing her hence appears unrealistic. Rather, Bundy seems to have been drawn to a specific body type, roundabout age and ethnicity (Caucasian).

Is it plausible that Bundy let a potential victim go who had seen his face, possibly learned his name, may have seen the license plates, could definitely describe the interior and exterior of the car?

Going off of what I wrote above, Kritsonis further suggests that Bundy must have been stalking her previously to picking her up at the bus stop: She states that, at Bundy's request, she removed her hat and Bundy asked why she had cut her hair. Even if he had "missed" the day of her hair appointment, he would have had to follow her on the day of the abduction, because without doing so, Bundy would not have been able to seek out the Renton bus stop, as an opportune location to lure her into his car. This means the only way for him to know her exact whereabouts would have been lying in wait in front of her home, following her until she had reached the bus stop. Would he not have seen that she had cut her hair? Would strands of her short bob not have peeked out from underneath her hat? Wouldn't he at least have seen her walk past a window in her apartment while he was stalking her?

Washington resident Drew Bales alerted me to the fact that he'd looked up snow days in Renton for the year 1972 in order to determine when the reputed kidnapping had occurred.

According to him, the event would have had to take place in January. Washington state was experiencing one of the worst snow storms in its history, so much so that Seatac Airport was shut down, as were many schools and businesses. And yet another local researcher, Eden O'Brien, explained:

"As someone who lived in Renton and knew someone who went to Renton Tech., I know absolutely everything is closed down during a medium to heavy snow. The buses stop running during as well. Where I live now [city redacted] we close the city down for any snow. In Tacoma, it has to be a heavy, icy, snow. Renton is between the two."

Enraged about Kritosnis' hair, Bundy purportedly drove her to the university, where he managed to open the door from the inside without effort, despite the missing door handle... He proceeded to shove her out of the car onto the frozen ground right on campus, and in broad daylight.

The fact aside that it's questionable whether the school was even open that day, if it was, as she insists, then we must remember that a college campus is busy all throughout the day and through much of the evening. We are asked to believe that Bundy risked 1) having an entire college campus witness the event 2) giving these witnesses time to note down his license plate and 3) banking on Kritsonis not going to the police, together with all witnesses who would have corroborated her story.

Of course, Kritosnis did not file a report with the police after almost being murdered and having to at least ponder that Bundy would likely have moved on to another target. The other prospective victims' lives did not matter to her. Add to this Kritsonis' own speculation that Bundy must have stalked her prior to the abduction. Meaning he knew where she lived, knew which bus stop she went to on a daily basis. I'm not aware whether Bundy asked Kritsonis where her college was located so he could safely drop her off in front of its doors. Considerate killers certainly are a shocking rarity. All sarcasm aside, I do wonder how that interaction went. If she had to provide him with the location of her school, it wouldn't have been a stretch of the imagination that he wasn't all too familiar with the area. Why then did she not give Bundy the address to the next police station instead?

It seems there were many missed opportunities, and while shock, fear and confusion may paralyze some victims while living through a traumatic event, it is beyond my comprehension why Kritsonis didn't at least go to the police after the ordeal, since Bundy may have also simply just waited half a year – until her hair would've grown back – to finish the job.

Lastly, Kritsonis states she saw Bundy a year and a half later on TV and "realized she had escaped a serial killer."

A serial killer?!

He wasn't known as a serial killer at that time, which, from the timeline she gave us must have been in 1973. A time he had not even started killing for all we know.

It was not until August 1975 that Bundy was first arrested by Utah highway patrolman Bob Hayward. It would take even while longer until Bundy's face first appeared on the national news. Because of all of the above, I personally remain in doubt about Kritsonis' Bundy abduction.

When this chapter was but an article on my blog, I received this comment shortly afterwards:

Dan Kritsonis says:
August 17, 2019 at 3:03 am
Edit

I

Sotria is my sister. It was Bundy. 100%. You didn't see the look on her face when she saw him on TV.

★ Like

understand Mr. Kritsonis' natural impulse to want to defend his sister. I commend him for having done his best in acting on his conscience, which was certainly somewhat influenced by a sense of family loyalty. In the end, since Mr. Kritsonis was not present during the alleged crime, his word is as good as his sister's. Kritsonis' reaction shocked Dan and, perhaps, appears to be enough for him to verify her account. It cannot be enough for students of the case however. Research doesn't stop at the awkward and hard questions, it begins there.

A look of fright on someone's face, or the fact that someone is related to someone is not indicative of them being correct in their assessment that it was indeed Bundy who attacked this person.

Likewise, I want to direct the same question towards Mr. Kritsonis I asked earlier:

Why did he not motivate his sister to go to the police to help prevent further attacks and to truly try and help his sister remain safe? After DaRonch's abduction, patrol cars were increasingly seen in the neighborhood.

From my detailed analysis above it is evident that pivotal elements of her story cannot have occurred the way she states. Ted Bundy may have likened her attacker. Due to not remembering him correctly or entirely, she may have transferred his face onto the man who offered her a ride at the bus stop, and I will go into further detail about such widely spread occurrences and accidentally false identifications later on.

Mitzi Bader Erb's Story

Mitzi Bader Erb is a woman who claims to have also been present at Lake Sammamish on July 14th, 1974. It was that sunny and blissful afternoon when Ted Bundy abducted Janice Ott around 12 P.M., and Denise Naslund about five hours later. The interview was uploaded by the channel *"Mason Weaver Is Clarence Mason"* on August 31, 2018. The description entails the statement that she "survived" an encounter with Bundy, an assertion that in and of itself ought to guarantee many clicks, but that is factually incorrect.

The interviewer introduces Bader Erb by stating that she escaped Ted Bundy as a pre-teen because she had had "the right mindset."
This alone could be viewed as a slap in the face of every single victim of Bundy's, as it suggests that they were either too careless or too gullible to save themselves. Nothing could be further from the truth.

Now, Bundy did have two twelve-year old victims, namely Lynnette Dawn Culver (Idaho) and Kimberly Dianne Leach (Florida), and six others were between 14-17, including the unidentified Idaho hitchhiker.
We must remember that Culver, judging by the last photos taken of her, appeared two to three years older than she was. Having the appearance of a 14-15 year old, Culver certainly would fit into the age bracket of Bundy's targeted victims in Utah. Leach was a chance abduction and was blindsided by a much more brazen, and much less competent version of Bundy. Bundy had slipped into a mindset of utter kill despair. He could no longer attract victims with his looks and charm, the way he had grown accustom to before his incarceration.
This initially led me to conclude that Bader Erb's allegation may not be entirely reliable. In January 2020 though, Bundy fiancée Elizabeth Kloepfer re-published her 1981 autobiography.
Her daughter Molly contributed her own chapter at the end of the book. In it, Molly recounts several chilling events between her and Bundy. These events involve variations of verbal and emotional abuse, and at times the painstaking admittance of physical and sexual abuse. Bundy's may hence not only have been a *hebephile* and *ephebophile* but a *pedophile* in the actual sense of the word.

When the interviewer asks Bader Erb what occurred that day, she vividly recalls details of what the areas surrounding the lake looks like. She is able to describe leisurely activities, being able to "hang out" on the beach, wait in line at the concession stand, or ride your bike through the nearby woods. As soon as the questions move to Bundy, she doesn't seem as confident: Bader Erb is unable to recall whether she and her friend Laurie were arriving, returning or leaving the lake area, intimating there may have someone else to accompany the girls.
She appears to be stalling further by remarking feeling unwell that day, and mentions a horse that she had intended to sell.
Instead, she talks about anything and everything except for the actual encounter with Bundy. It would have been beneficial for viewers had Weaver asked who else the other person, that may or may not have been at the lake with the girls that day, actually was. An eyewitness, it seems, that could have added their perspective, and who got lost in the convoluted narrative entirely.

It goes further downhill from that point on in the interview: Did she see a sailboat or not when Bundy pointed at the parking lot? What were the circumstances of him approaching her and her friend Laurie? She can't really say and is visibly struggling for words.
A few sentences earlier, Bader Erb had remarked that she didn't remember if she was getting back to the lake or not. At about four minutes into the interview, she suddenly states she and her friend Laurie declined Bundy's request for help because they had to go home. If there is any truth to that claim after all, it could be expected that it was (early) evening by that time, so sometime around or shortly before the Naslund abduction.

Bader Erb's uncertainty about the entire scenario would be more believable if she had never heard about Ted Bundy's case before now, and she was asked to recall an insignificant event involving an odd stranger. This would account for the lapse in memory, decades later. But she concedes she learned who he was "a year or less than a year" later while watching footage about Bundy's arrest.

The next red flag is the phone call to her friend Laurie which she mentions afterwards. She exclaims, "*Wow, oh my gosh, that was Ted Bundy!*"
A rather perplexing notion, considering it implies notoriety when Bundy wasn't yet infamously known as a serial killer at that time.

It's exasperating that the most pressing question seems to never be asked by interviewers

of such alleged survivors: *"Why did you not feel the responsibility to go to the police?"*
Police could at any point in time have used further clues about Bundy's whereabouts and demeanor in order to put together a more coherent timeline of events.

15-year old Sylvia Meixner, née Valint, whose case I will outline later in this publication, was encouraged by her father to immediately contact Seattle PD. Both of them possessed the clarity and conscience to do their civic duty.

And even Elizabeth Kloepfer reported her suspicions about Bundy being the "Ted" from Lake Sammamish to Detective Hergesheimer, although she was officially engaged to the man and vastly struggled with a guilty conscience and severe self-doubt.

Bader Erb further relays to us that Bundy's eyes, upon their refusal to help him, "immediately changed color." (Here we go with the supernatural myths again.) In fact, he became "instantly angry," within a split second of the girls' refusal to aid Bundy. This is not what we know of Bundy at all however. He remained charming and calm when approaching women, very aware of not acting out so as to draw attention to himself after a failed abduction.

(The exception to the rule being his odd demeanor at Viewmont High when he attempted to convince Raelynn Shepherd to follow him outside and ultimately taking chance victim Debbie Kent after DaRonch had escaped him earlier that day.)

Anything else would have raised the prospect victims' suspicions, prompted them to ascribe possible sinister motives to him asking for help. They would have remembered his visage more clearly had his demeanor left a negative impression on them, and Bundy was fully aware of this. Bundy could also not afford to let the mask slip on July 14th as the lake area was packed with thousands of people; he did not need witnesses within earshot that would attest to Bundy becoming upset.

And why would he have reacted so scornfully, considering there were plenty of other young women he could have chosen from? He had done the same on other occasions, as the statements of co-eds such as Kathleen Clara D'Olivo, Jane Curtis and others prove. If anything, Bundy was a rather patient hunter during that time.

As I mentioned in one of my articles, Bundy had not attacked minors in Washington either. This change in victimology was likely borne out of necessity; he wasn't familiar with the Utah landscape and needed victims easily controlled. Naïve teenage girls were ideal for his purposes. The change in victimology also prevented law enforcement agencies to suspect that the "Ted-"killer was now operating in two states.

Lastly, Bader Erb confirms that she was usually someone who would have helped anyone at any given time, she had declined to help because she was on her way home. So

34

it had, as was claimed earlier, nothing to do with her being "in the right mindset" of having picked up something insidious about Bundy.

In short: The entire interview not only makes no sense but is one vague mess of implications and "memories."

The point of this entire interview doesn't seem to have been to share a brave tale of survival. The imperative part was the "moral of the story," the video's final warning to be mindful of your surroundings, and develop a keen awareness of stranger danger.

I would agree that these are solid skills to develop and practice at all times. However, while the video's message is an admirable sentiment, it would not have needed the – possible – creation of yet another Bundy abduction story to drive that point home.

Victoria L.H.'s Story

Victoria L.H.'s book – or rather leaflet – *"Conquering The Haunting Memories Of Ted Bundy"* contains 30 pages of her alleged encounter with serial killer Ted Bundy, and how it influenced her later life. Merely 21 of the 30 pages contain actual writing. The font is large, spaces between words and lines are wide. Her story would fill approximately seven pages of a Word document.

L.H. intimates that sometime between 1969 and 1970, when she was fourteen or fifteen years old, Bundy drove past her while she was out on a walk. This event took place in an area close to UC Berkeley in Piedmont, California.

Bundy supposedly hollered and leered at her as he drove past the girl. He turned his car around so as to drive past her once more, his genitals flopping out of his pants as he leaned outside the window to get her attention. Now, we are aware that Mr. Bundy was an exceptionally athletic man but not a contortionist with skills otherwise only found in *Cirque du Soleil* entertainers.

Although the author was only about ten minutes away from home, she decided not to run back to safety. Instead, she proceeded on her merry way while being sexually harassed. L.H. launches into an illogical explanation that, because there was a turnout, she then voluntarily climbed into the passenger seat of Bundy's car while Bundy's "little Bundy" was still merrily flopping around.

The killer, she writes, appeared rather threatening and *"as if he was the devil himself."* And why wouldn't one volunteer to go on a nice little drive with the Lord of the Underworld after all.

Bundy proceeded to tell L.H. that his girlfriends all called him *"Teddy Bear Bundy,"* something completely uncorroborated by any of his girlfriends, friends or family. At least one of them, one might think, knew of this uniquely cuddly nickname.

Pointing to his genitals, he remarked that *"somebody is very happy to see you,"* while *"making sure that his penis was waving around out of his pants."* A penis waving around all on its own! Now this is something the world had never seen before until that point in time. Contortionism is nothing next to that, indeed.

After a short while L.H. allegedly developed the courage to tell Bundy that she *would* get out of this car right there and then and that he *would* let her. And what do you know! He did, stating *"My reputation must precede me."*

A wise remark for an offender to make, providing his prospect victim with the opportunity to report to police his insinuation of notoriety. If only all of Bundy's other victims had known of this neat little trick of just *demanding* to be let go. Thus concludes L.H.'s tale of brave survival.

When talking to a law enforcement officer on the phone to give a statement in relation to her above experience, L.H. remembers telling the call taker, *"He just tried to kidnap, rape and assault me!"* Did he now! I must have missed that part what with all the penis waving contortionism in the narrative.

The officers on duty relayed to L.H. that the bespectacled man with the bleached blond hair (?!) in the red (?!) Volkswagen Beetle was in fact a known rapist whom they already had in their system.

This is a daring statement to make because not only is there no file of Bundy in relation to any rapes, but no file of him exists in relation to any other confirmed crimes in the area either. The only possible overlooked rape we are aware of is the one perpetrated on Washingtonian resident Martha Feldman in 1974. (Available in the Files Section on *CrimePiper*.)

Despite Bundy primarily engaging in auto theft during his youth, the notion of the red VW remains questionable as we have plenty of witness accounts confirming that he used his own tan VW Beetle from 1974 on until his first arrest in 1975. (>Utah, DaRonch case.) L.H. may have taken the idea of a bright orange or reddish-orange VW from reading about the killer's last known vehicle, which he had stolen from one Rick Garzaniti in Florida in 1978.

What is verifiable is that Bundy did visit San Francisco in May 1969 in an attempt of reuniting with his ex-girlfriend Diane Edwards. Since L.H. states that *"It was a sunny warm Saturday or Sunday"* the day Bundy made his abduction attempt on her, the time frame and overall area is also congruent with his known California visit. However the story itself and what allegedly followed, are not. Additionally, another visit to San Francisco was made in early 1970, likely January, ergo we can exclude it as a possibility.

The police agreed to L.H.'s "terms," as she refers to them, of not letting her parents know about the encounter because they would *"never let me out of the house again by myself.*" And why not after all. A known rapist on file certainly shouldn't bother anyone, least of all the police who are by law obligated to alert a minor's parents regarding any crime planned or perpetrated on them.

Police did not entirely keep their word though, because approximately a week after the alleged abduction attempt, L.H.'s school counselor pulled her aside to ask whether she had "*recently* [been] *involved with the police in a crime?*" Just as the police had done before her, the counselor displayed great understanding in L.H. being averse to her parents learning about her Bundy encounter. She promised not to involve them. In fact, the counselor revealed, the police had already been deliberating how to go about concealing from L.H.'s parents that she would have to give an official statement at the precinct. Finally, they had settled on organizing a class field trip to the Oakland police station during which they could inconspicuously pull L.H. aside to interview her.

The forensic psychologist at the station who showed her a mug shot (?!) of Bundy's and further interviewed her is quoted as having said,

"*He has been charged with rape already in our system. […] [H]is girlfriend* [ann.: Diane Edwards] *dumped him. He's obsessing over it. You happened to remind him of her because your hair is parted in the middle.*"

Firstly, we already established that Bundy was not known to the California police at that point in time, so no mug shots existed.
His alleged "obsession" with Edwards is a Rule-ism; Ann Rule's 1980 (auto)biography, "*The Stranger Beside Me*" sparked the tedious myth of the "dark hair parted in the middle"-victimology as it pertains to Edwards.
Additionally, Bundy's juvenile record had been expunged at age 18, in 1965.
His first recorded crimes took place in Washington, and police districts were not co-operating by way of VICAP yet, since it simply hadn't existed yet. (>Keppel, Ressler et al, 1985.)

During the course of the interview, the unnamed forensic psychologist remarked that Bundy was on his way to becoming a serial killer (?!) and inquired whether L.H. would like her name to be included in any future books or movies about Bundy. Following this exchange, the entire police department began cheering and clapping for her, with L.H.'s classmates watching on in awe.

So we have forensic psychologists assuming the role of Hollywood agents, and her entire class witnessing that L.H. received standing ovations for something the classmates would have certainly not only have questioned her about extensively, but which they absolutely would have told their parents about. Who *may* just have contacted L.H.'s parents about this highly dramatic field trip.

Years later, while living in San Diego/California, L.H. was eventually stopped by a police officer who addressed her with,

"Hey girl! Are you the one that ran into Ted Bundy about ten years ago up in Oakland? [...],"

He prattled on that he had already been trying to find her for a while, at the request of a movie producer who wanted L.H. to play herself in an upcoming production about Ted Bundy. The Hollywood producer in question had found out about her due to one of her former classmates turned actor who'd recommended her for the role. It's important to note that by that time she had no contact to the classmate whatsoever.

The entire Hollywood portion of the story grows ever wilder but as it is only marginally related to Bundy, I shall not dive into it any further.

What all of this indicates, however, is that Victoria L.H. seems to have a unique perception of reality. Others have remarked that she sounds like a pathological, albeit not a skillful, liar.

On page 21, the author writes,

"I ended up with needing several minor surgeries along with one major surgery that all in all left me chemically unbalanced and emotionally out of control."

A chemical imbalance leading to emotional instability could, in my opinion and as far as I am aware due to my reading, indicate a prior head injury or neurosurgery.

In her mid to late thirties, the author claims that, practically from one day to the next, she went into a state of Ted Bundy-amnesia. She was incapable of remembering the encounter or her colorful Hollywood experiences. Not even despite occasionally reading about Bundy in the newspaper did she recall that she had met the murderer years earlier.

These memories only reappeared once she also remembered that she was sexually abused as a baby.

A problematic statement in and of itself, as the brains of infants up until the age of about 3-4 years old do not possess the ability to form memories, particularly none that would be accessible as an adult. Considering that all these alleged memories resurfaced during the 90's, my assumption is that L.H. may have fallen victim to – or was in part influenced by – the *"Michelle Remembers"*-Satanic Panic.

The author concludes her leaflet by sharing that she was 53 years of age at the time of publishing. If this is correct, and one may be inclined to believe her as most people at least remember their date and year of birth, then she was not 14-15 years old in 1969-1970, but eleven years old. This mathematical error takes away even more credibility from her alleged survivor story.

In my personal opinion, L.H.'s writing style, the serendipitous events and her naive worldview all denote magical thinking, however deliberate or involuntary it may be.

Debbie Harry's Story

Debbie Harry, lead singer of the punk-pop band *"Blondie,"* is adamant that Bundy attempted to abduct her in *"the early 70's."* Although she had remained firm about this statement since the late 1980's, a recent 2020 interview now quotes her as saying that the event took place in 1970 sharp. Harry also mentions that this incident occurred long before she was active in any band.

Her story took place in the late evening hours in New York City's Village neighborhood. Harry attempted to hail a cab to head to an after-hours club.
According to Harry, a little white car pulled up next to her after circling the block several times. The driver finally stopped to offer her a ride, remaining persistent until she relented. Upon climbing into the passenger seat, she immediately noticed his foul body odor.
She is quoted as saying that was aware of how unbearably hot it was inside the vehicle. It was then that Harry observed that all of the windows were rolled up despite the heat of the summer evening. When she moved to roll down the window, Harry realized that there was no inside door handle in the car, and that the entire back of the car was stripped out. There were no back seats, no panels, nothing.
When Bundy allegedly noticed that Harry was in the process of rolling down the window to try and reach the outer door handle in an attempt to escape, he violently yanked the car around to turn a corner. Possibly to have her slam back into the passenger seat. Instead Harry was catapulted from the car and Bundy simply kept driving, leaving her behind on the asphalt.
Approximately fifteen years later, Harry saw footage of Bundy on television and realized that he had been the man who nearly abducted her.

There's already a problem with the year(s) given, because Debbie Harry joined the folk rock band *"The Wind in the Willows"* as a back-up vocalist and tambourine player in the late 1960's, releasing the band's only album with them in 1968. That she was "not yet in a band" at the time of her Bundy experience simply cannot be true. Likewise, Bundy's whereabouts up until 1968 are well accounted for, and it would be years before he began his serial killing activities.
Bundy's curriculum and the jobs he worked on the side did not allow for expansive

travel between the late 60's and early 1970's. We know he had a dedicated list of employment from 1968-1972, which gives reason to believe it was not likely he was in New York at the time of Harry's accusation. His obligations were as follows:

- Valet at the Seattle Yacht club from September 1967 to January 1968,

- Safeway Stores stocker from April 1968 to July 1968

- Bus boy at the Olympia Hotel in 1968

- Campaign legwork for Governor Evans and aided in Art Fletcher's campaign during the entire summer of 1968

- Delivery man for Legal Messengers, Inc. from 1969 to May 1970

- Delivery Man at Ped Line Medical Supplies from late 1970 to early 1971

- Call taker at the Seattle Crisis clinic from September 1971 to 1972

- Therapist/Co-counselor at the Harborview Mental Health Center from June 1972 to November 1972

- Seattle Crime Commission from November 1972 to December 1972

As for his university studies, Bundy transferred to the University of Washington in 1968 in order to study Chinese, an endeavor he aborted several months later. Instead, he enrolled at Temple University in Philadelphia while visiting family in Pennsylvania. During that time he may also have visited Burlington, Vermont to procure a copy of his birth certificate. He returned to the UW to study psychology and remained in Seattle until September 2, 1974 when he moved to Utah to study law. So his movements across the United States have been thoroughly documented throughout these years.
Is it possible that he went to New York City while visiting with his family in Philadelphia without telling anyone, without us being aware of it? Perhaps.
Why this seems highly unlikely, however, is the fact that Bundy habitually purchased gasoline, or much of anything else, via credit card. There are no credit card statements or

gas receipts that place him anywhere in the big apple or the state of New York at any given time.

Harry does not identify the "small white car" as a VW. Bundy's infamous tan Beetle was purchased from one Mrs. Martha Helms in March 1973. Before that he owned a blue VW.
Bundy may have stolen or "borrowed" a vehicle; he had after all racked up an impressive juvenile record for breaking into cars to take them on joyrides. His mother had aided him in having his record expunged when he turned 18, so it would not influence his later college choices and career.
A stolen vehicle is also far more easily detected than serial murder, and Bundy remained free of auto theft charges until the mid-70's. We cannot determine it with absolute certainty, but it's at least questionable he would have dared steal a car during that time frame as it may have led to the discovery of his murderous acts. If that holds true, then this further indicates that it was not Bundy who offered Harry a ride.

From all those who are confirmed to have eluded Bundy, as well as witness statements from Lake Sammamish, it is known that Bundy was not in the habit of acting persistently, but rather nonchalantly, easily backing off from one potential victim to try and secure another. Anything else could have drawn negative attention to him.
So while he may have been adamant Harry enter his car, it would have been a deviation from his usual behavior.

It is difficult to accept that Bundy had a pungent stench about him in light of what everyone who knew him personally has confirmed about his obsessive-compulsive cleanliness and neatness.
His apartments were unusually spotless for a man his age, as Utah Detective Jerry Thompson once remarked while in the process of searching Bundy's abode for evidence. Even his hangers were evenly spaced apart in his closet.
Elizabeth Kloepfer, Bundy's fiancé, did not mention once in her autobiography "*The Phantom Prince*" that Bundy ever struggled with personal hygiene either.
Now, the term "body odor" is of course a very general one and we must also take into account reports of Bundy allegedly having reeked "like burnt carpet" or even "sulphuric" while being interrogated, so being highly stressed.
I shall once more point to my previously mentioned article, "*Metaphysical Myths & The Entity*" which explains any and all of the above.

What is far more concerning is Harry's allegation that the inside door handle was missing. I have repeatedly written about this myth, which was debunked by the best and brightest Bundy researchers, but here's yet another thought that casts some doubt on this statement. If the inside door handle was missing, how did Harry close the door from the inside, not being aware that the door handle was not in place until she attempted to roll down the window? Bundy would have had to get out, open the door for Harry and also close it for her, yet this is not part of her story.

It is the next part which truly baffles. The fact aside that, had the window been rolled down enough to fit her entire arm and shoulder through it so she would be able to open the door from the outside, it would have been enough to let enough cool air in. In this instance, it would have made more sense to ask the driver to roll down his window a few inches to achieve proper air circulation. There was no need to roll down the window all the way, but of course the story would not quite work without this crucial detail.
I have looked at weather charts from the summer months between 1970-1972, the average temperature being approximately 75°F, so a somewhat moderate temperature. Unfortunately Ms. Harry has not provided us with a specific date, and only a roundabout time frame for what would have been a traumatic event in her life. But we know that she was on her way to an after-hours club, so it must have been later in the evening when temperatures had already somewhat dropped. How hot could it have been in the car in that case?

My friend Katie Marcrum helped me recreate this scenario with her own 1968 VW Beetle. Additionally, my mother and I did the same with her vehicle. I'd like to point out that none of us was driving at the time, the car was parked. I also strongly recommend not re-enacting this stunt while driving.
It was entirely impossible for me to reach my arm through a crack in the window without my head being in the way and bumping into the roof of the car.
In order to bend my arm the correct way to reach towards the outer door handle I had to have my shoulder outside of the car window, and even then I could not reach the door handle. But the window sadly sustained a crack because I had to shift my weight downward. Only when I had rolled the window more than halfway down was it possible to reach the door handle.
Now, I must take into consideration the fact that Harry stands at 5'3 while I am 5'8 ½ and that with approximately 102 pounds she also weighed less than I do. It may be possible

44

that when she leaned outside of the window, which she would have had to, it was left undamaged. Her head and shoulders would have still made reaching out of the window to pull the latch of the door handle impossible.

The next problem I encountered when the door did open was that being in the position I was in, it was impossible to control the swing of the door. The door swung open with me clinging to it and I was pulled outside, my feet barely on the floor of the car anymore. Had my mother been driving I would with almost certainty have ended up underneath the wheels of the car.

Another question I asked myself was how fast was Bundy driving? The speed limit in New York City in the 1960's-1970's was set at 30 mph/~50 kmh.

Investigating accidents involving people exiting a car while it was in motion determined that it would have been very questionable that Harry would have gotten away without injury or with only scrapes and bruises. (Which she did not mention sustaining after her adventurous stunt.)

Certainly, Ms. Harry would have had to check into an ER or a doctor's office in order to determine whether she had suffered any internal injuries or fractures, and yet she does not report having done so either.

Lastly, here is a thought that kept popping into my mind about the reported encounter: Would Bundy not have taken great glee in relaying this story to investigators on the eve of his execution? He had begun confessing to murders, some of them in chilling detail. He even went as far as confessing to murders no one had linked him to, such as Pocatello/Idaho victim Lynnette Dawn Culver or the unidentified Idaho hitchhiker. He had even confessed to Bob Keppel the murders of three additional hitchhikers in Washington and one in California.

For someone as narcissistic and grandiose as Bundy, a high profile victim such as Debbie Harry would, I believe, not have gone unmentioned.

Diana Fishbein's Story

In March 2019, WJACTV uploaded an interview with Diana Fishbein to their website. Fishbein was a neuroscience and criminology student at FSU, Florida State University at the time she states she met Bundy.

She told reporter Samantha York that she was sitting at a coffee shop, when she noticed a young man who would relentlessly stare at her. He did not seem like a customer as he had no beverage or food in front of him. She experienced him as "creepy," yet tried her best to ignore him.

The next day, she returned and found the young man sitting there again, for the second time without a beverage. She notes that his eyes were black and insinuates that he looked "non-human." All in all, she intimates, she saw the man two or three times, eventually deciding to avoid the coffee shop for a while.

This particular coffee shop, Fishbein's home, the sorority house and Cheryl Thompson's abode were all within several blocks of each other.

Several days later, she learned of the Chi Omega and Cheryl Thompson attack, and when photos of the suspect were released she realized that Ted Bundy had been the man who had sat across from her.

Fishbein says, *"All my doors and windows were open, I was home alone the entire evening, half a block away,"* insinuating that she may have been a target, although Bundy appears not to have followed her outside the coffee shop on either occasion.

From the WJACTV website:

"Given her area of research studying the minds of psychopaths and killers, Dr. Fishbein knew some of the police officers in Florida when Bundy was taken into custody. She recalls, "One of them told me that when he was arrested, that he said to the officers, 'I have an uncontrollable need to rape, mutilate and kill young girls. Somebody should study me.' And I wanted to be that person because I was already interested in psychopaths and he was the ultimate psychopath." She adds that her experiences with Bundy gave her a personal tie to her studies, "I'm absolutely fascinated with people, individuals that are literally born without a soul, that have no conscience, that have no moral compass.""

Now, Fishbein's story is more difficult to examine because of its brevity, yet not short enough not to raise several good questions.

For one, while it is not impossible, it is very unusual that a coffee shop would permit someone to remain on the premises without purchasing a beverage or food item. Bundy, according to Fishbein, stayed long enough to make her uncomfortable, and she does not report that staff approached his table to take his order or ask him to leave. Coffee shops in university districts are known to be lucrative, buzzing hotspots. Does it make sense that they would let someone hog a table for a considerable amount of time?

Secondly, why would Bundy not purchase a drink to better blend in? This seems out of character for someone who, at the time, had done everything in his power not to raise suspicion. He lived on stolen credit cards in Florida, and had no viable trouble getting by, so a coffee would not have broken the bank.

Drew Bales, Bundy researcher of 30 years, noted that a coffee shop in the U district, which police and security personnel are also known to frequent, seems to be a very curious place for a convicted felon to casually hang out. And that is indeed a very valid point.

On the other hand, Bundy wasn't shy enough not to be seen at the Sherrod's nightclub where he was spotted by multiple people who testified this to police after the Chi Omega attack.

Here's where the story spirals a bit: Bundy's alleged admission that he was a rapist and murderer who could not control himself.

From the Pensacola Transcripts, which are also linked in the Files Section of the *CrimePiper* blog, it's evident that Bundy was more than reluctant to admit to any guilt to Don Patchen and Norman Chapman. He did not even want to give police his real name before Washington attorney John Henry Browne advised him to reveal his true identity. From every police file, every interrogation and interview, we know that Bundy compulsively played mind games with investigators and prosecutors, and only gave up some – not all – details about his murders within the last days prior to his execution. Could law enforcement officers other than Patchen and Norman have delivered this quote to Fishbein? Certainly. Merely, it is doubtful that Bundy himself said as much.

Linda Lail's Story

In February 2019, the National Enquirer ran a story on another alleged Bundy survivor by the name of Linda Lail, then 67 years of age. Until 2018, Lail had worked as a registered nurse. Originally from Vancouver/Washington she now resides in Ocala/Florida.

What makes Lail's story special is not only the fact that she is supposed to have been one of Bundy's first victims, but that he attempted to abduct her twice within a five year span.
In 1969, Lail was on her way to work her waitressing job at a local restaurant when Bundy approached her. She states,

"He was handsome but creepy. [...] He sweet-talked me into his car. He pulled out handcuffs and showed me a police badge. I started to struggle, and he hit me. [...] My boss from the restaurant rushed over and pulled the door open."

As Lail ran to safety, Bundy allegedly smashed his vehicle into several cars while escaping.

Five years later, in 1974, Lail lived in Des Moines/Washington with her husband. He was at work one evening when a man made an attempt at opening the partially open sliding door which was yet blocked with a broom handle for security.
Lail screamed in fright and slammed the door shut, trapping Bundy's hand between the door and its door frame. She intimates that he eventually managed to break free and ran off into the night.

If Lail was 67 years old in early 2019, she was born in 1951 or 1952, making her about 16-17 years old at the time of the alleged abduction attempt.
She may have worked an after-school job, at least it is unlikely that she had dropped out of school because she trained to be a nurse several years later.
From Bundy's activities in Utah we know that he absolutely targeted minors, yet the timeline is off for this particular modus operandi of his.
Bundy's early attempts at targeting women were rather unsuccessful. In 1968 he jumped

on a female co-ed's bed, immediately fleeing the scene when she began to scream. His first two recorded crimes were indeed home invasions, he broke into Karen Sparks Epley's and into Linda Ann Healy's basement rooms.

Before that, however, Bundy tried his hand at blitz attacks several more times. While in Philadelphia in 1969, he rented a hotel room under a false name, planning to overpower a woman on the way into her room in order to rape her. His nerves got the better of him and so he never carried out the attack.

In 1972, he attacked two women in short succession. One he clubbed over the head with a piece of wood while she was about to enter her home late at night, but she, too, screamed and Bundy fled. The second woman he hit from behind while she was about to unlock her car. Her screams equally scared him off.

From this we can gather how inexperienced Bundy still was, how easily deterred by a woman's scream. His modus operandi was still underdeveloped, and so he had not yet learned to wear the mask of superficial charm, not thought to use an injury or authority figure ruse to make the women and girls follow him to his car willingly.

There is no indication that Bundy ever used the authority figure ruse before moving to Utah, where he used it on survivor Carol DaRonch, possibly on high school drama teacher Raelynn Shepherd, maybe even on Debra Jean Kent and Melissa Smith. DaRonch remembers that he showed her a police badge and also presented a firearm, and it may be that Bundy obtained both items at a Halloween store during a clearance sale, as it was a little over a week after the Laura Ann Aime murder that he kidnapped both DaRonch and Kent.

It does not appear remotely possible that Bundy showed Lail a badge and hit her over the head with what we may assume was a crowbar, as this was his go-to weapon since 1974. He had possibly starting using it on the night of the Donna Manson murder, maybe even Healy, but definitely not yet in the case of Karen Sparks on January 4, 1974.

When we discussed this case in one of my study groups, someone suggested that it sounds problematic that Lail was on her way *to* her job, yet her boss ran *out* of the restaurant to rescue her. Did he see her arriving, although she had not arrived at work in her own car? How small was the parking lot in that case?

I would add that it makes little sense for Bundy to drive a potential victim to her job, only to attack her on site, in a parking lot with possible witnesses present.

Another question is how severely Bundy had beaten her – not enough to require medical assistance it appears. But why did she not go to police? Did neither her boss nor her parents, whom I presume she lived with as a teenager, drag her to the precinct if not at least to a hospital?

Now, the most pressing thing to ponder when taking a look at the second alleged Bundy attack is how precisely Bundy would have found Lail.
She had gotten married, and it was common that women during the 70's still assumed the last names of their husbands. Since she had moved to a different city, Bundy would have had to keep close tabs on her whereabouts during all of these years. Was he camped outside her house every few days, taking notes as soon as he saw her packing up the house to move? And why would Bundy lie in wait all of these years without finishing the job?
Bundy stalked at least two of his Washington victims, Sparks and Healy, for a longer period of time. It appears that he had been trolling them, learning where and with whom they lived, their hangouts and routines while already actively planning to murder them. There is a world of a difference between observing a victim to determine the ideal time and place to abduct her, and stalking an escaped victim over years, who might very well spot and recognize him from a previous encounter and alert the authorities to his presence outside of her home.

Furthermore, it would have been a welcome addition to include how long this struggle at the door lasted. It sounds as though it was over within seconds. Barring sliding doors with broom handles for security was a known practice during that time, and is to this day where I live. But what interests me is where was Lail when Bundy sought to unlawfully enter her house? The logical approach would have been to wait until she was out of sight or at least with her back turned towards the door. Opening the door as slowly and quietly as possible makes even more sense. Bundy could of course have done all of these things and Lail turned around or re-entered the room just in time to see him standing at the door, rushing to it in order to swiftly shut it.
Of course, we know that Bundy did not have a grievous hand injury in all of 1974, which he would have sustained had things transpired the way Lail reported them.

Now, if we go back to the duration of this frightening encounter, we must let it play out in our heads. I re-enacted this scenario as well, and assuming both the role of Bundy as well as Lail on two separate occasions.
In all fairness, there are more than technicalities to consider, though. Most significantly, I

of course know my mother's face and was in the advantage that I was aware of precisely what was supposed to ensue and my role in this re-enactment. In that sense, our experiment lacks one pivotal factor and that is the surprise one.

Which is exactly the point on the other hand. Because during a burglary attempt that would very likely not have lasted more than seconds, up to a minute at best, Lail insists that she recognized a man she had had one brief interaction with several years ago. A man who was known to frequently change his appearance, his hair style, facial hair, style of clothes, who disguised himself with hats, mustaches and glasses. A man who would have looked drastically different five years later, which photos confirm.

How long would it take, during a violent struggle, to get a good and firm look at his face, a face that was likely contorted with anger and later pain, all while he did his best to break into Lail's abode?

Where would her eyes have been? Most likely not on his face but on his hand attempting to push open the door, perhaps even trying to grab and hold on to her. So while the attack lasted longer, eye contact will likely not have.

In conclusion, could Mrs. Lail have been attacked twice by two different men? This seems more plausible.

Janla Carr's Story

 In the third installment of the FBI report, available via print and on the organization's website, there are several pages involving the testimony of a woman named Janla N. Carr, born on January 23, 1952.

She contacted the FBI between 1990 and 1991, stating to investigators that she was Bundy's half-sister on her father's side.

Carr claimed that Louise occasionally took Bundy with her to meet Janla and her father, and that Louise was introduced to her as "Aunt Eleanor." During these encounters which began when Carr was approximately between four and five years of age, her father was often so "mean" to Louise that little Bundy asked why he was treating his mother so badly.

In 1956, during one of these visits that took place in West Park, Pittsburgh, the children departed from where the adults were sitting, and Carr allegedly watched an approximately eight or nine year old Bundy push a toddler off of the embankment and onto the train tracks. The child's mother allegedly witnessed the event. After the murder, Carr insists, Bundy attempted to rape her.

Now, this cannot possibly be true. Whilst Joshua Goldstein from the *Max Planck Institute for Demographic Research in Rostock*, Eastern Germany, helped analyze mortality data in order to prove that male children have been reaching puberty earlier in the last few decades, he determined that the average age of males reaching puberty in the 1950's remained constant at approximately 12.5 years of age. From this we can conclude that Bundy would not have been physiologically capable of raping anyone at this tender age.

What is far more disturbing and demands further probing is whether the murdered toddler's mother did not immediately try to confront Bundy, to force him and his parents to accompany her to the nearest police station. Did the mother not scream, cry, utter any loud human – or inhuman – sounds at the sight of this horrific sight? Would those wails not have been heard by people in or near the park? Yet no police report of the time identifies a mother whose child was murdered in front of her eyes in the fashion described by Carr.

Carr is adamant that Bundy had a twin brother. Those leaning towards believing Carr posit that Louise may have taken turns taking Bundy or his twin to these family reunion meetings with the Carrs. One person even suggested that it may have been Bundy's twin who later sought out Carr in Pittsburgh.

Obviously this logic is flawed. This isn't *"Breaking Bad"* and we're not talking about the Salamanca twins but real life.

The fact aside that the Lund Home did not record a twin birth in Louise's case, why would Louise not have brought both boys to meet Mr. Thomas Dowling Carr and his daughter Janla?

Where exactly was this twin brother when Bundy grew up in the Cowell and later Bundy household?

Where is he on any family photos that found their way onto the internet over the decades? He should have been in at least one photo together with his twin.

And where is he now? If he resembled Bundy, just imagine the terror and panic that would have followed, had he been spotted someplace after Bundy's conviction, let alone after his execution. He would be the most (wrongfully) arrested man in the history of the USA.

Bundy, Carr further claims, had approached her while she was on a trip to Vermont in 1968, and had begun visiting her in Pittsburgh between 1969 and 1970 while she was a student there. She had at first not recognized him in Pittsburgh because her father and Bundy had "brainwashed and hypnotized her to forget his face."

Bundy continued to confide in her that he had committed several murders, among them one in Tacoma and another in Pittsburgh, where he had allegedly stabbed to death a co-ed while visiting Carr. He had allegedly also claimed responsibility for murders in Kettering/ Ohio, and boasted about being responsible for shooting a man in Jackson/ Mississippi, resulting in a race riot, which bears certain Manson-esque connotations. (Helter Skelter.)

Before claiming that he had psychic powers, proving it by "making her forget everything he had ever told her for many years," he allegedly also confessed to the murder of little Ann Marie Burr, though Burr's name is not explicitly mentioned. Rather, she is described as a little girl that Bundy, then fifteen, pushed off of a bridge, resulting in a broken neck, and whose dead body he sexually assaulted afterwards.

Without giving details, Carr also identifies Bundy as responsible for the 1969 Turnpike murders in New Jersey, although the case of Elizabeth Perry and Susan Davis remains unsolved.

Bundy had allegedly intimated to Dr. Ron Holmes that he had killed the two women, yet no recording of it exists. It is noteworthy that Bundy was incarcerated with Gerald Stano at the time, who was a suspect in the case and may have filled Bundy in on several details of the double homicide.

Carr, like many others, appears to conflate both Bundy facts and myths in order to lend more credibility to her accusations.

Her father admitted to investigators that his daughter had never mentioned Bundy prior to his execution and categorically denied knowing Louise Bundy. Janla, he said, had in fact spent a great amount of time meticulously researching Ted Bundy, reading any book available on him, as well as studying any newspaper and magazine article she could obtain.

What is most interesting about Mr. Carr, who was incidentally born in Ohio in 1913, is that one of his longest employments was at the railroad mail service.

So we have here the Bundy connection to Ohio that his daughter appears to have fabricated, and to her father's occupation due to the toddler murder story.

The question is why Ms. Carr would create such a false narrative, and whether she did so deliberately or because she was mentally confused.

The latter may have very well been the case, for Carr recounts that she used to consume LSD when out partying. LSD, while not generally harmful, may have disastrous effects on the brains of those with certain psychiatric predispositions. Serial killer Herbert Mullin was known to extensively experiment with hallucinogens, likely contributing to his later delusions of hearing God's voice, instructing him to kill random individuals in order to prevent earthquakes that he believed would otherwise kill thousands.

Carr had inexplicably stopped attending classes on a regular basis, only to drop out of college after two semesters. Afterwards she appears not to have worked but isolated in her apartment, paid for by her father.

Add to this that Carr suffered from what her father ominously described as "thyroid problems." Individuals with thyroid disorders may in some cases develop cognitive dysfunction and affective disorders.

For instance, over-activity of the thyroid may result in anxiety, under-activity may result in depression. Both may lead to insomnia, extreme mood swings, aggressive behavior, a short temper, as well as a multitude of other mental and emotional disturbances.

Although the phenomenon is rare and poorly understood according to the *National Center for Biotechnology Information*, they may also result in psychotic episodes.
I'm obviously not diagnosing Miss Carr, but the notion of her thyroid problems and later removal could explain why she so suddenly struggled in school, changed her entire behavior and began developing the incorrect belief (non-bizarre delusion) that she was related to Bundy.

The point of examining cases that ring obviously false is to illustrate how profoundly such accounts alter and interrupt the investigative process. They may even interfere with the psychological evaluation, and the so-called "profiling" of the offender.
Police are legally obligated to follow up on every single report, every possible lead, and are called to even investigate stories that sound outrageous and ridiculous. For one, this takes time. It also involves reaching out to these alleged victims' or witnesses' family members, to other possible eye- or ear-witnesses, along with establishing the complete timeline of events, contact law enforcement in different cities, districts, states.
And in Carr's case it also involved attempting to determine Bundy's parentage and whether he had a twin. This costs precious tax dollars, but more importantly, the work load, the paperwork, the stress for investigators is unimaginable.

Several months before publishing, I stumbled across an old newspaper article on Janla Carr's death on February 1, 1997.
After she had been released from another stay at a psychosocial hospital, Carr had been found dead in a subway tunnel known to local police as a hangout for the homeless and what local police referred to as "bag people." Police commented that although Carr had not been homeless, she had yet been known for her "eccentricities." Friends of Carr's had stated to law enforcement that she had seemed happy after her release, yet she had also stopped taking her medication.
Due to a lack of defensive wounds, signs of sexual assault or any other traces of violence, her death was ruled a suicide or accident; the medical examiner's records list the cause of her death as "undetermined."

As though her death at age 45 was not tragic enough, her father Thomas D. Carr died in a bizarre public spectacle on the one year anniversary of his daughter's death.
According to the *Pittsburgh Post-Gazette* and *North Hills News Record*, Carr had not taken well to Janla's untimely demise, developing paranoid delusions that his daughter had been murdered by the FBI and that they were now also looking to murder him. He based

his belief on a torn piece of paper on which Janla had written 19 years earlier that a strange man in her apartment had gotten up from the couch to look at her in an unsettling way. Police note Thomas Carr became obsessed with this piece of paper.

Ultimately, he entered a Walmart where he talked to a phone equipment clerk about how his phones were tapped by law enforcement, that a neighbor had murdered his daughter and had broken into his home to steal his stamp collection. He further accused the perpetrator of having called "the woman he was in love with" to play the recorded murder of his daughter to her, resulting in the woman never speaking to him again. Carr kept calling police that day and revisiting the Walmart store. Lastly, he shot himself in the chest three times, dying on the premises before paramedics arrived.

Mary Conely's Story

Mary Louise Conely, born September 24, 1954, resides in Jacksonville/Florida. On June 11, 2019 she launched her brand new *YouTube* channel, dedicated to her unconfirmed Bundy encounter which, she estimates, took place sometime in mid-June. Conely admits to having read many a Bundy book, among them Dr. Al Carlisle's "*The Violent Mind*," as

well as Robert A. Dielenberg's "*A Visual Timeline.*" On a social media profile she states that she studied Accounting and Criminal Justice at NFU.
She has since told parts of her story on the Quora website as well.

It is at times a tad challenging to make sense of her account due to what I personally view as disorganized speech.

I will share several longer quotes in order to illustrate my claim, while otherwise retelling the above referenced entry. In order to facilitate a smoother reading experience, I have enhanced the below paragraph by adding correct punctuation and Italic font to indicate direct speech. It begins like this,

"Mrs Sexton had some issues, ok. This is the then aging mustang. [Ann. She included a photo of a car at the beginning of her tale, which I have omitted in this publication.] *Note at one time Debbie's mom tried to breed German Shepards. See the fence chain link? I had written in my diary of the encounter. I was between Kathy's and Debbie house, Debbie said you can't, your mom will read it. I ripped that page out and put in pipe of fence. I think forensic could still bring it out cause it was written hard.*
When I was 12 soon to be 13. I wanted to get to Junior High ahead of time."

It is at that point entirely unclear who Mrs. Sexton is, which the reader learns many pages later is her friend and fellow unconfirmed survivor Debbie Hogue's mother's last name.

Just as much a mystery is why a forensic team would be interested in a fence's pipe. The remark regarding the diary entry is no evidence, if I may for one moment remind of the infamous *"Hitler diaries"* that German news magazine STERN ("Star") purchased for 9.3 million US dollars after historian Hugh Trevor-Roper had authenticated them.

STERN sold serialization rights to several German newspapers; the entire nation was in uproar. Later, however, a man named Konrad Kujau was found to have forged the diaries.

As for Conely's diary, it's possible she wrote the entries as a teenager. Which still doesn't have to make them true necessarily.

Likewise, the photos she provides are completely unrelated to the Bundy encounter and do not substantiate her claims.

Conely adds unusually many details to her story, such as what she and her friends were wearing on the day of the unconfirmed abduction attempt, what J.E.B. Stuart Middle School was shaped like, what the name of her music teacher was.

In short, there is a lot of insignificant information to dig through until one gets to the relevant Bundy parts of the story:

On June 16, 1967 Conely and her friend Debbie Hogue, both twelve years old at the time, started walking home from school. They stopped at the baseball bleachers to sit down for a spell.

Conely told her friend she would "pretend" to hitchhike, sticking out her thumb. Mary "Magic Memory" Conely describes several of the car models, including their colors, that allegedly passed them until a new, bright red VW stopped next to them after Conely hollered at him, *"Hey, Naked!"*

The shirtless driver got out of the car to speak to them, and Hogue entered his car, sitting down in the passenger seat.

Because Conely didn't want to let her friend go alone, she joined them, climbing into the backseat.

Upon noticing a stack of books in the backseat, she blurted out, *"There's books,"* to which Bundy allegedly replied, *"Just move the books."*

Eventually, Bundy produced a revolver from the glove box, but it is unclear for what purpose or if this action was followed by a remark of his.

Conely claims that upon asking his name, Bundy replied that it was Theodore. (A name Bundy detested, instead insisting that everyone call him Ted instead.)

Conely writes,

"This seems silly, but when he said 'Theodore,' my kid mind thought 'See a door,' which of course – there is no door in the back of that type car. I asked, "What's your last name?" He said Bundy. I said, "Your name is Bundy like my clarinet, and your gun is silver like Debbie's flute."

Let's take note: Theodore – See a door – there is no door – your gun is silver like Debbie's flute.

Now, while there is indeed a company named Bundy which has been producing musical instruments since 1948, this entire sentence construct is a classic example of *word salad*, whether the encounter or exchange occurred like this or not at all.

Conely further states,

"I chatted on, Debbie's father (even though her mom and dad were divorced), I told him Debbie's dad is an Admiral at NASA which was true, but divorced.
I remembered her dad Mr. Hogue he had a piece of material called Teflon he said would be used in

the Astronauts' suits.

I also talked up her older sisters, so pretty more his age. He was about 20, he had a mole or two on neck. He had a tan. There was golf shirt on floor.

Also he had eyebrows that seemed to go across forehead. I thought his eyes looked black, there was a stink in car like unwashed hobo sweet, crappy stink.

He drove us to Harlow and Blanding, not far, to a gas station, red brick, it was red brick back then.

Debbie got out, I just prayed she would open the knob latch on seat to let me out. I KNEW THIS WAS BAD. I wrote about it in my diary.

   […] Later that summer, when my aunt and grandmother came to visit, these are the frayed imitation pull on jeans. Same jeans, and the diary.

I thought he might be from the Navy base cause his hair was short cut even, even across the back neck.

Also it was an out of state tag. New VW Bugs were kinda rare. I gradually ended my association with Debbie. She took advanced courses to get out of HS fast and she was kinda wild. The tag on the VW was tan, seemed like dark numbers but can't remember.

Off the top of my head it was like white with black digits and a black line around the edge, I tried to always remember this event because of the gun being displayed. I'm damned lucky.

The man Theodore had a look at that time 1967 like a young Rob Lowe. Also Debbie handed him a note.

The VW color red was bright, but not fire engine red, that's too much orange, it was a touch of crimson, shiny new, like would be hard to match that red. Blood drop red…"

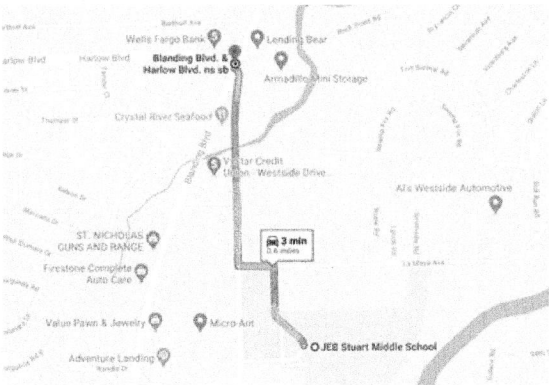

Google Maps, 2020

Obviously, Conely continues to speak about unrelated issues in a mostly disorganized manner until returning her focus to the Bundy encounter.

Although Bundy reportedly preferred knives in order to intimidate and subdue his victims, we know from Carol DaRonch that he employed the use of a gun in her case. However, why did Bundy even pull a gun on the two girls, what was said, what were his intentions? Why would he threaten the girls with a weapon, only to pull into a gas station in the middle of the day and give them ample opportunity to evade him? Why did Hogue write Bundy a note, did Conely never think to inquire as to what was written on it?

Conely speculates that one of Bundy's relatives or friends had joined the Navy to avoid the Army or Marine Corps, and that being on tour, he had lent Bundy his vehicle. To say that this is a stretch is an understatement. This speculation leads us ad absurdum just as much as the suggestion would that Ted must have been a vampire because he had a sallow complexion.

And indeed, Conely later recants to provide yet another theory: He must have leased the ruby red VW with his scholarship money.

It appears that Hogue introduced Bundy to her mother and sisters who made a big secret out of it. No explanation is given why Hogue would introduce someone who had threatened her and her friend's life with a gun to her family. Is Conely implying they were dating? Did the note that Hogue handed to Bundy include her phone number and/or address?

Most importantly, why would her family keep Bundy visiting their home a secret? It seems almost as though Conely was implying the family knew about Bundy threatening the girls, and yet it is unimaginable that they wouldn't have immediately called the police as soon as he set foot into their home.

Many pages later, Conely intimates,

"In the VW, he was not wearing a shirt. I figured he had been playing basketball by the pine trees, there was a yellow golf shirt in the rear. His shorts weren't sporty. The we're like tan golf shorts. Tailored Bermuda shorts. Dress shorts tan."

Although she at first insisted that he must have played basketball by the pine trees, she later concedes:

"You know I've been on this for months, no one will confirm. But in the dawn hours over night I figured something out. Remember he was shirtless? And there was a sour crappy smell. I've realized he wasn't playing basketball. He had had sexual activity, he was only going around the trees and baseball field in an effort to get back to highway 21, Blanding to points north and west.

He probably stayed in a cheap motel after his sojourn to Florida, then picked up a hooker, street walker, then dropped her off on the Westside, maybe at Dorminy and Wesconnett.
She says just circle around J.E.B. Stuart and you'll head straight back to Blanding.
He saw us playing around, and he almost lost it. Thank God he came back. He dropped us off just off Blanding. He did not want to get lost, he was either headed out or needed to catch a flight or pay for room. Not one single person has helped me, but this makes sense. Can you imagine the odds."

Conely closes prosaically,

"All I know I what I saw and thank God no harm came to us. He said his complete name. I saw his face. It was void. like the sea or night sky, evil unibrow."

We may take note, unibrows are evil. Power to the face wax. Conely is now going full Cesare Lombroso on her readers. Austrian (Italian) criminologist Lombroso (1835 to 1909) was an "expert" in phrenology, namely the practice of determining the inherent goodness or evil of people due to the size of their cranium, which was later taken to the extreme when the matter of Eugenics became relevant across Europe, and people's heads and noses were measured in order to determine whether they were Jewish or any other type of so-called "*untermensch.*"
Needlessly to point out, almost any of his findings have been successfully debunked over the past few centuries.

I will save myself the trouble of delving further into the "theory" that Bundy's alleged "sweet hobo stink" was caused by prior intimate relations with a lady working in the sex industry.

Now, as for the reason that neither Hogue nor Conely reported Bundy to the police, the latter is of the opinion that all law enforcement would have done was take an incident report and patrolled the area around the nearby schools.
Which, one would presume, is still how law enforcement operates, as this is how offenders are frequently apprehended.

Conely's attempts to prove that Bundy was in the area at the time entail further speculations mainly based upon the inflation rate between 1967 and 2019, and the allegation that the University of Stanford paid him to travel to Daytona/Florida in 1967.

Why they would have done so or what she bases this opinion on remains a mystery to me.

Although the late Ann Rule had written in her book, *"The Stranger Beside Me,"* that Bundy did not enroll at Stanford until 1968, it can indeed be verified that he spent late June through August at Stanford until returning home to Washington. A drive from Stanford to Daytona, or alternatively Jacksonville - where Conely resided at the time - would have taken over 40 hours.
On the other hand, a drive from Tacoma to Florida would have taken approximately 44 hours, so there is a rather insignificant time difference.
The argument that Bundy must have made his way to Florida while in Stanford because it was closer to his kill destination is essentially nil and void.
Bundy could have just as well traveled to any other state, to Canada, to Mexico during that time by that logic. Even during his weekends or days off from college, it is questionable that he would have taken a drive this long on the offhand chance that he may encounter a victim there.
His pattern remained constant in terms of abduction locations. He killed within one state and any surrounding states, as is the case in Washington (Oregon victim Kathy Parks), Utah (Idaho and Colorado victims). He did not travel across the country just for an "Entity experience" because it was simply not necessary to do so. It would in fact have been a risky endeavor.
    Although this was Conely's only alleged encounter with the serial murderer, she wrote seven and a half more pages of irrelevant details about her teenage life in the 60's, including what one would typically want for Christmas, and that female children were typically given a night gown as well.

Because of this, she intimates,

    "[T]he little girl [ann.: Ann Marie Burr?] *wore the night gown with panties, and the Healy girl wore one too, but Ted Bundy removed hers, so as not to look at it. His own sisters probably got the ubiquitous gift also."*

    Conely delivers no explanation why Bundy would not have wanted to look at female nightwear, and neither he nor any of his girlfriends ever made a mention of it either. There's nothing in any of the interviews, literature or official records suggesting this. We must hence dismiss this interpretation as it appears to be baseless.

In between asking herself whether Bundy cried when watching Bambi, Old Yeller or the news about President Kennedy's assassination, her opinion on his psychopathy can be summed up in one side sentence:

"Did he decide to go Republican not because of CODIS but because he did not like all the emotion around him."

Does she really mean CODIS? I shall contend myself with sharing this excerpt from the fbi.gov website:

"The Combined DNA Index System, or CODIS, blends forensic science and computer technology into a tool for linking violent crimes. It enables federal, state, and local forensic laboratories to exchange and compare DNA profiles electronically, thereby linking serial violent crimes to each other and to known offenders. Using the National DNA Index System of CODIS, the National Missing Persons DNA Database also helps identify missing and unidentified individuals."

Conely additionally speculates about Bundy's pseudonyms used in Florida, Chris Hagen and Richard Burton.

Because Jonathan "Jon Jon" Hagans, three years of age, went missing on June 11, 1968 from Jacksonville Beach, Conely is of the opinion that the strongest suspect must be Ted Bundy.

Firstly, while the family names Hagen and Hagans are similar, this is not indicative of Bundy having been involved in the possible abduction of the boy. Not only was Ted Bundy a heterosexual *erotophonophile* (hedonistic/lust killer), was thus exclusively interested in female victims, but he had returned to Washington in late February 1968, taking on a stocking job at the Queen Ann Hill Safeway grocery store in April, where he worked until late July 1968. We face yet another timeline issue, and must remember that it would have taken Bundy around 44 hours to drive to Florida. At least there are no flight records that show Bundy having taken a plan to Florida within this time frame. Additionally, while some speculate that Bundy chose the name Chris Hagen due to his alleged fondness of the movie "*Black Christmas*" (1974), we must take into account that Bundy had a habit as stealing ID's and credit cards from young men, such as Florida State University student Kenneth Misner, taking on their names. Lastly, the antagonist's name in the "*Black Christmas*" movie was Chris Hayden, not Hagen.

It may be tempting to ascribe a hidden or conspiratorial meaning to these "Bundy coincidences," yet facts and logic speak against it. In a case spanning over many years, with around thirty known and by far more speculated victims and survivors, there are bound to be coincidences or repetitions of a sort.

As mentioned in my *CrimePiper* article, "*Ted Bundy: Curiosities and Coincidences*," Bundy's life was marked by "bookends of murder" as researcher Jennifer M. White once referred to it in The Ted Bundy Research Group.

Although I see more evidence to the contrary, if Bundy's first victim truly was little Ann Marie Burr of Tacoma in 1961, it's interesting that her mother Beverly Burr's maiden name was Leach, incidentally Bundy's last murder victim and also a minor.

Bundy was born on the 24th of November, his daughter was born on the 24th of October, the day of his execution was the 24th of January, his inmate number was 069063, whose digit sum is 24.

In short, it is us who ascribe meaning to dates, times, names and numbers. Certain first and last names were more common during the 70's than they are now, and certain numbers stand out not because of a conspiracy but because discussing the case each day of our lives, we are more sensitive to such coincidences, noticing things that others typically would not.

Now, as for the name Richard Burton, Bundy also did not choose that name for himself. Rather, he stole a firefighter's vest with that very name attached to it prior to the abduction of Kimberly Dianne Leach on February 9, 1978.

Yet again pointing to my above mentioned article, it's a curious coincidence that the actor Richard Burton starred in a movie called "*The Sandpiper*," incidentally the name of the tavern where Bundy and his fiancé Elizabeth Kloepfer met at. And just like Richard Burton, Bundy had loved a woman named Liz.

So Conely's allegation that there is a deeper and sinister meaning to Bundy's alias Richard Burton, who also happened to be the name of a British author (1821-1890) that translated the Kama Sutra and according to her "*also oddly published a book on pederasty*" is not that odd at all.

The name Richard gained popularity in between 1930 and 1946, with between 30,000 and 60,000 male infants being given the name. Meaning that in the sixties and seventies chances were increased one would encounter a young male with that very first name.

In conclusion, I'd like to address the issue of Conely's closing statement, "*I believe God had more for me to do.*" This assertion is echoed by former Kloepfer friend Marylynne Chino, who in a KUTV interview, published on the channel's website on July 25, 2017, said,

"I'm lucky to be alive. Why not me? I don't believe people who say he wouldn't hurt people he knows. I don't believe it. Why didn't he hurt you? My honest answer, I think, I had more to do in this life that's the only thing I can tell you."

And then there is the tale of an unnamed Chi O sister who allegedly stated to Father Kerr, a Catholic cleric who was called to the crime scene on January 15, 1978, that Bundy was obviously deterred from raping and murdering her because she had prayed the rosary before going to bed.

As Alex R. Hey noted on the *Epic Pew* website, the story first appeared in a 2002 *Pittsburgh Newspaper* article and did not resurface until it was mentioned in a 2009 *"third-hand account"* blog in 2009.

The blog in question, *Bett Net*, is owned by Domenico Bettinelli. He learned of this event in 1994 via his friend Frater Gabriel, an acquaintance of Monsignor Kerr.

Now, neither Conely's nor the above mentioned persons' remarks ought to be dismissed lightly. They are exceedingly tone deaf and cruel. Their message is not one of hope and faith but one of judgment, centered around the belief that the deceased and surviving victims were viciously assaulted because they lacked faith or "right" religious denomination.

It is neither for Ms. Conely nor for any human being to determine this. The "right" faith would be compassion, kindness, empathy. With this audacious condemnation of the victims, Conely – as well as others making such outrageous statements – make it appear as though they had little to no empathy with the victims and the plight of their families at all.

On a last note, Conely went to Nathan B. Forrest High School in Jacksonville in the early 70's, the same high school Leslie Parmenter went to in the late 70's. Some have suggested that if Conely's story is fabricated, she may first have heard about the abduction attempt of Parmenter's in high school, where such tales gain infamy and are usually shared over many years among fellow students, new and old. They believe that Conely may have taken Parmenter's story, her "fame," as inspiration for her tale.

If that is correct however, one must wonder why Conely chose to only now share her account. Perhaps because had she shared it back then, there was enough evidence to prove her wrong, or because her friend Debbie Hogue would not have corroborated the story?

Richard Marquardt's Story

Within the last two years, I was made aware of a man who had contacted author Kevin M. Sullivan to have him write about his Bundy survival story, and who has been speaking about his ostensible Bundy ordeal in various relevant *Facebook* groups.

The below quotes are taken from a thread started in October 2019 to which he replied. I believe it is necessary to show them in their entirety and without paraphrasing. Although most Bundy aficionados are well aware of his real name, I have chosen to use a pseudonym to do my part in avoiding he be identified and possibly harassed online. Be advised that I underlined the passages that directly contradict each other to make them more easily identifiable to readers.

"Labor Day fell on September 2nd in 1974. My block several miles off I- 84 in Boise was dead, really dead that Day. I went for a walk taking a break from the Jerry Lewis telethon. I ended up in a post office dumpster a few blocks from my house. I was inside this dumpster when he [ann. Ted Bundy] attacked her on the street between this post office and my house.
Minutes later I made a really bad decision and yelled over to a scene I couldn't see. I could see the front of the Volkswagen only but not any more. He silenced her right then in an instant.
Minutes after that he met me and confronted me. We had a 10 minute encounter that changed me forever. Too long a story for Facebook posts. But she was real, and when he admitted killing her toward the end of his life, he wasn't lying. But he did lie about the circumstances and I know how it went down."

He continued,

"I'll tell you [ann.: the group] a little bit about her. She fought hard, she was blindsided by a psychopath. She had a good heart and spirit and I believe, I truly do, that she became my wonderful guardian angel.
I never saw her face. I only knew she was there and she knew I was there. By the time I realized what was happening, I'd already made mistakes. It pains me greatly that her identity was never found. So much so that I've decided to write about it. So much so that after all these years I've decided to talk about that day. I was nearly killed myself [and] I never spoke about that day to anyone."

And further,

"I have a lot to say about her, but I don't know who she was at all. Only that I heard her screams and knew she had been killed because of me. I know exactly where she was killed and I know Ted lied about that day."

Kevin M. Sullivan was quick to spot Marquardt's comments and chimed in to relay to the group,

"Here's what Richard Marquardt said when he contacted me about this supposed encounter with Ted Bundy: "I'll give you a short run down on this [by] phone. It sucks but it's the phone I have on messenger. So as I best remember it would be Sept. 2nd 1974. A week and a day after my 9th birthday.
I'm coming home from whatever I was doing and the Volkswagen pulls up in front of me. Considering the spot it does make sense he timed it to go down there.
He asked me to stay back a bit from the car. He asked where all the girls are and I judged his age and so forth and told him about a local park where college aged adults always hang out. He didn't care for my answer and continued with questions about girls around here. He asked if I had an older sister, he asked if I knew any of the girls in the neighborhood?"

Now, above is what he said today. Now, folks, be warned: [Richard] can't even get his stories straight!"

Mardquardt directly addressed Mr. Sullivan in his response:

"You would have a complete story had you ever been interested or given me the time of day. One thing I do need to convey though. At the time I first contacted you I didn't have my complete memory back yet. I suppressed how the story began and was as amazed as one could be that intentional memory suppression can and does actually work if the situation is emotional enough. I did it and I did it intentionally many, many years ago. But one day I was writing in Ukraine last winter, and I was thinking about how strong the feeling was that he plunked her over the head on Jean street.
It was odd, it was an unnaturally strong feeling that I knew more but couldn't remember. I stopped writing for a minute and calmly thought about why I feel like I know more than I remember. Sure enough it came back like a wave. It's weird, it's not like I truly forgot something so obvious. Something I knew so completely.

Intentional memory suppression works or certainly can work. Anyway what I suppressed was the beginning of the whole thing. I did that in order to justify my actions. I did that because of guilt. Suppressing the beginning was the only way I could live with the fact I did nothing to stop him. I didn't call police until May of 1975, perhaps even June."

Previously, Marquardt had claimed that he had *"won his little game though and blew his mind."* Bundy blogger Rachel Neave inquired as to what precisely he meant by that. The reply came swiftly, *"His game (and he showed me what I can only assume was the monster saved only for victims). And it was horrific! I stood there and stared him down for a long, long time. [...] I've filled out a form online with the FBI. Probably in February of this year." [ann. The year was 2019.)*

Kevin M. Sullivan ended the debate with another quote from their previous conversation,

"Here was Richard's motivation for making up this stuff (again, from his contact with me.) "Making it into your book is not exactly my intention here." Did you get "not exactly?""

There's obviously much amiss with Marquardt's stories. Hedonistic lust killers like Bundy target those they are sexually attracted to as intimate activities with the living or expired victims are their primary goal. Ted Bundy was heterosexual, so naturally he targeted females. As a male, Marquardt does not fit that profile.
Of course, if we take into account that Bundy would have eliminated Marquardt because he didn't want any witnesses, that would be a fair addition; alas, Bundy let the boy go because Marquardt, nine years of age, "stared Bundy down." I'll leave it up to the readers of this publication to decide how likely they consider this statement.
Several months later, Marquardt assumed the position of administrator in yet another Bundy group on *Facebook*. In it, he posted:

"Okay, so I hope this will be well received by the group because I'm going to begin my ramblings about my day. September 2nd, 1974. The day he abducted the Idaho hitchhiker. I'm the one person on earth that happens to know she was real. When he confessed about his murder, I can confirm it's no bullshit. So I have that.
Others perhaps looked into it a bit after his confession but I really doubt that investigation went very far. By the time he confessed it was 15 years later to a crime they had no idea if it happened or didn't. A quick search for locals is probably about as far as it went. So obviously we have to dig a

bit deeper than that.

I've come up with a theory. Follow along if you're interested and I'll show you how I came up with this particular girl. Feel free to add info if you might have a different hunch and we can explore who she may have been.

So, what exactly am I looking for? I believe Ted was constantly mixing lies with truth. A habit that became part of who he was. He wasn't just addicted to killing, he really struggled with the truth as well. Just an observation, I'm not trying to tell people who he was. You all know. To the point though there are certain things he said during the Idaho confessions that in all likelihood are very true.

Her age, yeah, he was probably honest and from what I heard that sounds right. Although I feel compelled to mention her screams sounded a bit older, very loud. But that's almost nothing, she had a slightly deeper voice than one would expect from 16-18. But she was under a serious attack so...

The green backpack. Absolutely true, saw it myself.

He got a bit elusive when he talked about where he picked her up and what direction she was going, so I don't hold any value to his claims here.

The necklace. I think he was recalling a real memory here and I buy it. The girl that fits all my criteria is wearing a necklace in her most popular photo that's a dead ringer for his description.

He definitely lied as far as not telling about coming into the city a few miles. Some might say it's not lying to just leave something out. Maybe true but when you're confessing to a crime, intentionally leaving out information could be considered lying. Just my opinion.

In all likelihood, and as I figured, in '74 after there were no reports of a missing girl in Boise I'm looking for a runaway or perhaps a girl recently released from foster care.

I've searched extensively nationwide for missing young women from '73 and '74. Not all but nearly all were straight up abductions. No way they were running around the Northwest hitchhiking with a green backpack. No, I'm looking for someone who left home on their own terms. I'm on the opinion Deborah Lee Tomlinson made it on her own for 10 ½ months before crossing paths with Bundy on the outskirts of Boise.

She's from a small town just south of Eugene which is also just about a straight line to and from Boise to anywhere East. So it fits nicely.

It's pure speculation as to her direction at the time and the possibilities are really endless without more info. But I can easily see where it's possible he promised her a ride downtown to the parks and pulled onto my block to abduct her long before they got downtown. Doesn't matter much but he did drive a few miles into the city. These are things that only I know. And I'm sharing because I think it's important.

Again folks, until I can get more info this is strictly theory. But I have to tell you it fits so far."

71

Commenting on his own thread, Marquardt later notes,

"Pretty weird update I didn't give enough credit to. I've found another interesting possibility about the identity of the Idaho hitchhiker.
Corrine June Groenenberg left home just two weeks after Deborah Lee Tomlinson. Corrine was from Modesto/California, and was also 16 years old with brown shoulder length hair. A family friend witnessed her walk from her home to the highway and begin hitchhiking. She was picked up by a man in a blue or green pick-up and was never seen again. I consider her much less likely and both girls would have had to survive on their own another 10 months but I have to throw her in the mix of possibilities.
Bundy claimed she was 5'6 with brown hair, between 16-18. By the time of the Boise abduction you could call them both 17. Deborah was just six weeks short of 17."

Attentive readers know by now that Marquardt did not only not speak about his day as he had promised, he actually revealed nothing noteworthy about the Idaho hitchhiker at all, instead producing word salad similar to that of Janla Carr, L.H. Victoria, Mary Conely, and Sara A. Survivor.

I'm not certain how one could ascertain from mere screams – and despite a complete lack of visual contact – that someone "sounds older" than their age. Marquardt had not heard the girl speak by his own admission, and had no way of comparing her speaking voice to her screaming voice. Moreover, it may surprise him to learn that some females do indeed have lower pitched voices even at a young age.

At the same time, how would Marquardt have spotted the green backpack if he was indeed hiding inside the dumpster, confirming for us farther above that he never saw the victim nor what occurred between her and Bundy?

What stands out is Marquardt's complex, possibly self-tailored, belief system. He insists the girl had a beautiful spirit despite not knowing her or even her name, and that she became his guardian angel.
Now, I refuse to argue metaphysics as they're irrelevant for our purposes here, so shall only remark that no dogma of any known religion includes the promotion of a deceased human being to "guardian angel."
Marquardt further insists that he is the only person to know the victim was real. I

surmise we are not counting the entirety of the Bundy community who are very well aware of the Idaho hitchhiker, or investigator Russ Reneau, who spoke to Bundy about the case.

Indeed, it was Reneau who elicited from Bundy the confession about the unidentified Idaho hitchhiker, including the tidbit that the girl had had a green backpack with her:

BUNDY: In approximately early September, 1974, I was driving from Seattle to Salt Lake City. I was moving. I was passing through Idaho on the highway . . . maybe it was 84 . . . the freeway. Somewhere just on the outside, very close to or on the outskirts of Boise, I picked up a hitchhiker traveling . . . well I was traveling east at the time. I'm trying to recall . . . she was standing down . . . it wasn't a downtown off-ramp, I mean on-ramp, but it was further out of the city. Ranch style suburban houses were in view of the off-ramp, on-ramp. It was early evening as I recall. Anyway, I pulled over . . . my car was full of stuff . . . she was carrying a large green backpack. I believe she was 16 to 18, light brown hair. about 5'6". My recollection is we stopped . . . well I had no place specific in mind, because it was after dark. It was

at that point of the freeway when you first come into any contact with the river. We were driving, somewhere we could pull off the side of the road and drive to the river, get off close to the river. The river would have been on the right hand side of the highway going west.

RENEAU: Excuse me you said west but did . . .

BUNDY: No that's not right.

RENEAU: OK.

Lastly, Polly Nelson addressed the hitchhiker confession in her 1994 book, *"Defending the Devil: My Story as Ted Bundy's Last Lawyer."*

Bundy had relayed to Nelson that he had been

driving around the hills of Idaho in order to familiarize himself with the area and discover convenient places to abduct females from.

He had allegedly not planned to take a victim on September 2nd, yet when he spotted a girl around fifteen years old, he invited her to sit down with him in his car to have a chat. She entered voluntarily and he immediately reached for the crowbar, rendering her unconscious. Because she awoke shortly afterwards, he struck her again, driving her across state lines (into Utah) and into a secluded place in some unidentified woods.

The girl must have been awake again at that point because Bundy confessed that he had "made her strip and kneel on her hands and knees," watching her cry and beg for mercy while he was taking Polaroids.

Ultimately, Bundy slung a noose around her neck, strangling her to death while raping her from behind.

A day later he returned to the crime scene in order to take more photos of her and dismember her.

   This is all that is known about the young girl. Marquardt believes that he can achieve what neither seasoned investigator nor citizen sleuth has been able to do – to identify her. How? By looking at missing teenagers who wore their brown hair parted in the middle and were reported to have had a green backpack on them. A backpack that they may have acquired after running away from home, if they ever did. Or a backpack they may have traded in for another.

As Dielenberg also notes in his book *"Ted Bundy: A Visual Timeline,"* the main issue with the Idaho hitchhiker remains that it's unclear whether she was a fabrication of Bundy's, created to try once more to stall his execution, or whether she really did exist.

If she existed, she was either not memorable enough for Bundy to recall her name, or he kept it to himself, just as he liked to keep details about Kim Leach to himself. He had struck the Idaho hitchhiker early on he'd admitted, preventing them from having a conversation about where exactly she was from and where she was headed.

Thus combing databases such as *The Charley Project, The Doe Network* or *The Murder Accountability Project* for young girls that may or may not have gone missing in the USA between 1973-1974 sadly appears a rather pointless endeavor in this specific case. There is no concrete evidence or reason why Marquardt would believe Deborah Lee Tomlinson "made it on her own for 10.5 months before running into Bundy."

Tomlinson, aged sixteen, ran away from home with a friend, occasionally identified as "a female friend." It is unknown where the two girls would have traveled to, nothing places them anywhere near Idaho in September of 1974.

As for Corrine June Groenenberg, the fourteen year old girl was from Modesto/California, and was last spotted climbing into a green or blue truck, driven by an unidentified male. Others have speculated that Groenenberg may be another "Santa Rosa Hitchhiker Murders" victim; indeed Santa Rosa victim Jeannette Kamahele was also last seen entering a truck resembling the one Groenenberg had climbed into.

Yet investigators cleared Bundy in Kamahele's case and have stated that they do not believe Bundy to be responsible for the Santa Rosa Hitchhiker murders either.

   I consider it doubtful that Groenenberg ran away from home as her mother had just been diagnosed with scleroderma, an autoimmune rheumatic disease, and the girl by all accounts wanted to support her mother and family during this time.

Barbara Webb's Story

In her autobiographical account from 2019, *"The Fight Of My Life,"* Barbara Webb intimates that she survived an encounter with Ted Bundy in 1965, when the killer was 18-19 years old and Webb herself was 21.

At the time she and her sister were working at a furniture factory in Portland.
One day, she took the bus and walked the rest of the way to the factory, located near the freeway, *"not realizing how desolate some areas would be."*
It was sometime in the afternoon and traffic was scarce when a *"light-colored car came slowly around the bend"* and stopped beside her.
Although Webb does not describe the man's facial features, hair or eye color, she states that he was *"extremely good looking"* with *"a twinkle in his eyes."* He rolled the window down to offer her a ride but Webb declined. Because another car was coming around the bend, he eventually had to move.
Apparently the young man had *"taken the freeway going south, gotten off at the first ramp to go over the freeway, and back onto the northbound lanes"* and returned to her, stepping out of the car and insisting – albeit still politely – that she enter his car. Because yet another car was approaching, he had to drive off again, but Webb had already grown scared and quickly made her way across the bridge towards the factory.
    Walking past a phone booth, she realized that it was occupied by a man whose back was turned towards her. When she turned around to try and get a good look at him, she saw that it was the same man who had asked to give her a ride. As he stepped outside of the phone booth, his face *"transformed into a hard and frightening expression,"* with his eyes glazed and looking *"like a demon straight out of hell."*
Webb did not give the man a chance to address her, briefly telling him that she had reached her destination before running towards the office door.
Co-workers offered to call the police for her, but she declined *"out of embarrassment."*
It's difficult to determine whether Webb is contradicting herself and mixing up timelines in the following passage. Which is why I'll share the passage in its entirety.

She writes,

"When they caught Ted Bundy, it was a shock! I was living in northern Missouri with no cable and only one channel on our television. I had been following the news, but hadn't paid too much attention to his appearance, until the day of his execution. At this time, he was shown walking outside, smiling, with a twinkle in his eye. At first, I wondered how such a vicious man could be so charming. But then, something else bothered me. A memory. I had seen that smile before! Some twenty years before! When the photograph was shown of how he looked as a young man, I knew that this was the same man! Why I was spared this horrible death, only God knows! But I felt that I must have a purpose in life, far beyond what I could see!"

Considering the overuse of exclamation marks and the various typos and grammatical errors in her book, it's possible that Webb didn't have a professional editor, and that she simply worded the above passage a bit strangely.

However, from the first sentence it sounds as though she realized sometime between August 1975 and 1976 that the man who may have attempted to kidnap her was indeed Ted Bundy, as it was then he was first arrested, and his case made national headlines, respectively.

Yet in the next sentence she relays to her readers that she did not see Bundy on television until January 24, 1989, more than 14 years after the alleged encounter.

More importantly, when analyzing her words, we must remember that Webb was on her way to work at a factory. The majority of factories in the 60's were closed on Sundays. That leaves Saturday as a possible day of the abduction attempt, at least if the attempted crime occurred before March 1965, the month Bundy graduated from Wilson High in Tacoma.

It is safe to say that up until March 1965 young Bundy will have been preoccupied studying for his finals and may not have had time or permission to leave the home for an extended day trip.

On March 29, 1965 Bundy was in a car wreck, likely Johnnie's car since Bundy himself did not own one. Although it's known Bundy had been arrested for car theft earlier in the year, had he crashed a stolen car, he likely would not have gotten off with a warning, which he did.

Webb doesn't give a date or month during which her Bundy encounter is supposed to have happened. She merely states that it was *"now into the year 1965,"* giving the impression that it was still relatively early in the year.

Bundy purchased his own first car, a 1933 Plymouth Coupe, on September 26th of 1965. However, looking at the color chart for 1933 Plymouth Coupes, it becomes evident that all models were painted in darker colors, ranging from grey to brown to black for the most part. No light-colored models were manufactured, meaning that either Webb did not encounter Ted Bundy, or Webb encountered someone whom she later incorrectly identified as Ted Bundy, or Ted Bundy stole a car to drive it to Portland and back to Tacoma – a risky endeavor.

According to Google Maps, the drive from North Skyline Dr. 658, Tacoma, WA to Portland, OR is estimated to take 2 hours and 27 minutes. We can assume that due to less traffic and a lower population density within cities one would have reached one's destination faster in 1965 in comparison to nowadays.

Yet at the same time we don't know how far Bundy would have had to drive within Portland to reach the factory.

And another factor comes into play here. Bundy didn't know Webb, wasn't specifically looking for her to abduct. So he was likely out trolling and may have already spent some time doing so.

He would have had to leave Tacoma very early and likely returned home late. Would Louise and Johnnie have permitted this? Particularly since it may have been Johnnie's Plymouth he would have been driving, and Johnnie partly worked weekends?

And lastly, would he have risked transporting a bleeding victim or corpse in his adoptive father's car at approximately age 18?

One final consideration is the issue of memory. The three short encounters would have lasted perhaps two minutes the way Webb described them in her book.

Would she have been able to reliably identify Bundy 10-24 years later, only from watching him on TV for mere seconds and due to the "twinkle in his eye?"

Sara A. Survivor's Story

In 2016, the book *"Reconstructing Sara: The Forgotten Victim of Ted Bundy"* was published by a woman calling herself "Sara A. Survivor."
Much of what she writes in her book can also be found on her blog, which I have listed in the *Sources & Further Reading* section at the end of this publication.
Sara's real name is well known to Bundy researchers from the Seattle Police Department files on Ted Bundy, also available on *CrimePiper*. The files include an array of her email requests to law enforcement regarding the Bundy case. It is hence unclear why she chose to publish under a pseudonym.
One thing sets Sara apart from most other unconfirmed survivors. She indeed went to university with a known Bundy victim, namely Georgann Hawkins. Whether the girls even personally knew each other or were indeed close friends, quasi-sisters, as Sara suggests, has never been corroborated. No photos of the two exist in case files, were used in any documentary that focused on the victims, or were provided by Sara herself to cement her claims.
Yet more difficult to believe is Sara's emphasis on having witnessed Hawkins' abduction, and that the girl was taken because she tried to prevent Bundy from continuing his frequent abductions and abuse of Sara. No confirmed eyewitnesses (Duane Covey, Steve Burnham, Jane Roberts et al) made a mention of Sara having been anywhere near Greek Row that night. They never made a mention of her period.
Plowing through the excruciatingly redundant memoir, which is equally rife with time jumps, was an arduous task. About a third of the book includes lists of apparent and alleged items found at dump sites that investigators didn't catalogue. Anyone who read Bob Keppel's *"The Riverman,"* knows how meticulously the young Detective and his team combed Taylor Mountain and its surrounding area for skeletal remains and any evidence that could have been relevant to solving the case. Thousands of items were collected, thousands of callers reported their boyfriends, co-workers, family members and suspicious neighbors to the police tip line. Thousands of sheets of papers were filled with details about the "Ted-" killer from Lake Sammamish... Yet Sara, it seems, ascribes sinister motives to the investigators, implying – as far as I understand – that the uncatalogued items are evidential of law enforcement being in cahoots with Bundy. That these investigators are also only mere human beings who were in over their heads

as the extent of the case became clear, is nothing Sara appears to factor into the equation. The *Ted Task Force* consisted of relatively few members. And, untoward as it may be, even investigators make mistakes, including misspelling names and losing evidence. If it looks like a duck, and quacks like a duck, it most likely is a duck.

Sara evidently remains unconvinced and continues to publish blog posts with titles such as, *"Ted Bundy Evidence Taylor Mountain: 158 items – Denied, Destroyed, Discounted For Decades," "Ted Bundy & The Public Image The Authorities Initially Created Of Him To Create Their Own "Super Cop" Scenarios," "Fact Check: Ted Bundy book, "Riverman" embellished, inaccurate, fraudulent," "2019/20 Ted Bundy Docs: Keppel Just keeps repackaging the case for his own personal profit."*

Some have speculated that Sara has such disdain for Keppel in particular because he was quick to refute her Bundy story allegations.

As for Ted Bundy, he almost seems like an afterthought in the *"Reconstructing Sara"* memoir. Sara insists she had lost nearly all memory of Ted Bundy, which returned to her in the years between 2001 and 2009. The author writes in detail about specific childhood memories, including which song was playing on the car radio while out for a drive or what she was wearing on a particular day but once Bundy is involved, her memory fails her.

A female author – clearly Ann Rule, though Sara avoids naming her – is allegedly responsible for some of Sara's false memories and earlier contradictory statements, which she now recants in her book.

Due to her PTSD-related "fragmented memory" – caused by head trauma that Bundy reportedly inflicted on Sara – there is no clear timeline established in the memoir. Instead, the author alternates between the years 1970 to 1976, frequently making contradictory statements that unfortunately don't facilitate the comprehension of what she is trying to convey.

Sara's childhood was marked by stalking experiences and sexual abuse at the hands of various older men, who, according to her, are responsible for her pre-Bundy memory loss and PTSD.

Around 1971, Bundy began calling Sara's private landline while she lived with her parents in Washington. He was a complete stranger to her. She did not know his name or what he looked like, and could not place his voice, although it sounded familiar to her. He offered her his counseling services – as so many strange men do over the phone – and in turn the teenaged girl willingly confided in Bundy all about her parents' difficult divorce, her loneliness resulting from it, and the fact she was often left home unsupervised.

Around the same time, Sara began modeling. She repeatedly points out in her memoir how beautiful and petite she was at the time. This seems to hold particular meaning to her, as though it validated her claim that Bundy had targeted her.

Bundy, she writes, came to stalk her at her tea room-, runway- and photography modeling jobs, yet she neither recognized him as the person who'd previously dated a friend's sister in California nor as the man who had approached her during a prior ski trip.

Sara is not certain when she first met Ted Bundy, but implies that one of two scenarios is most likely: In winter of 1970/1971 Sara, then a junior in high school, went on a ski trip at Crystal Mountain in the Washington Cascades with her friend "Robert." She attracted many a man's attention due to her beauty, and one of the men just happened to be Ted Bundy. "Robert" and Bundy had words though Sara doesn't recall why, but implies that both men may have been fighting over her. Approximately half a year later, "Robert" lost his life in a waterskiing accident. Sara admits to not having any real reason to think so but her *inner voice that has felt something was wrong back then* gives her the impression that Bundy may have sabotaged the ski or the boat to create the fatal accident. Why? Because he was jealous of "Robert."

Some of my study partners considered this a verification of Bundy lawyer John Henry Browne's 2012 KCPQ TV interview statement that the murderer had once confided in him that his first homicide victim had been a man. Others concluded that Browne may have taken "inspiration" from Sara's account, or that the two created their stories independently of each other.

Though Sara can't recall the rape, she knows it happened sometime between the skiing incident and summer 1971 when Bundy, whom she neither recognized as the man from the ski lodge nor as the stalker from her modeling jobs, visited her at home to play with her pet raccoon. He drove up in a cream colored Volkswagen Beetle. However, in 1966 Bundy sold his first car, a 1933 Plymouth Coupe, and bought a used 1958 Volkswagen Beetle of blue color. The purchase of his infamous tan VW occurred sometime in 1973. He did borrow his fiancé Ms. Kloepfer's VW on occasion, which was not tan in color but is recorded as being of blue or light green color in the case files of the King County Sheriff's Office.

Sara delivers other different occasions on which she was stalked by Bundy in 1971, casually noting that she was drinking heavily at the time. Bundy, she is sure, once followed her and a friend into the woods where the girls were taking a walk, another incident involved him breaking into her bedroom window while the entire family was asleep in the home. After spending time with friends in Modesto/California, Sara grew aware of the fact that the Santa Rosa Hitchhiker victims all bore a strong resemblance to her.

Readers of this publication may decide for themselves whether they agree. Below is a photo, taken from the Santa Rose Hitchhikers Murders website, of the victims; blondes, brunettes, raven-haired girls. Both confirmed and suspected victims include Caucasians, Polynesians, South-East Asians, Hispanic Americans, and those of mixed ethnicity. But they all look just like Sara.

Yvonne Weber

Maureen Sterling

Kim Allen

Jeannette Kamahele

Lori Lee Kursa

Carolyn Davis

Terese Walsh

Jane Doe

Before the sexual assault took place, Sara and Bundy went out to dance where he purportedly "measured" her hips, waist and size her with his hands. This leaves the impression that perhaps the Bundy Sara knows in her mind resembles "*The Silence Of the Lambs*" character Buffalo Bill. In fact, author Richard Harris based parts of this character on Ted Bundy, albeit not the part involving measuring girls' waists, which were inspired by serial killer Ed Gein, but the injury ruse M.O. employed by Buffalo Bill.

We find in Sara's book more of what appears in similar type accounts, such as Victoria L.H.'s or Janla Carr's. Public applause and validation. Whereas L.H. found herself in the midst of an entire police precinct applauding her bravery to identify Ted Bundy while on a school field trip, Sara was met with applause by an entire operating room of medical doctors who – hands dripping with blood – clapped and cheered when she shared with them the good news that she had become pregnant.

Wherever Sara traveled, be it to Vancouver, Oregon, California, as well as a myriad of places within Washington State, Bundy was already there. Stalking, watching, abducting and assaulting her. This would have been a full time job that would have left Bundy with little to no opportunity to spend as much time with the Kloepfers as he did, to attend his classes, work the occasional odd job, see friends and family, and lastly stalk and murder all of his other victims.

Both the female and male friend who could have corroborated Sara's stalking and victimization by Ted Bundy died. She chose not to name them or provide any further evidence of their existence.

Sara, much like others portrayed in this publication, may have survived traumatic events, either at the hands of Bundy, or by another person. It is equally possible that portions of her memories are real and true, while others are not. Evident is only that she, too, chose not to report these violent assaults on her during the years they supposedly occurred, and that what readers are left with include various segments of events that are lacking in logic, consistency and do not match Bundy's modus operandi. I will close with a question. If Sara admitted to having recalled and shared false memories before, is it truly a stretch that her memory of Bundy as her abuser is equally faulty?

Molly Kloepfer's Story

The updated and second edition of *"The Phantom Prince: My Life With Ted Bundy"* by Elizabeth Kloepfer, written under her pseudonym Elizabeth Kendall, was scheduled to be released on January 7, 2020.

However, on Christmas Eve of 2019, several single pages of *"Molly's Story,"* an additional chapter written by her daughter, were leaked on several social media sites.

As more and more pages were shared among Bundy researchers, one thing became painfully clear — Molly intimated she had been sexually molested by Ted Bundy as a prepubescent child, the man who had taken on the role of stepfather, albeit not legally.

Just days before the pages found their way onto the internet, twenty additional photos from the autobiography had surfaced, many of them depicting Molly and Bundy together, smiling into the camera, laughing together.

He was seen playing with her and her friends, teaching her how to ride a bike, cradling her in his arms, making faces at the camera while Molly was putting scrunchies in his hair.

The majority of us had been oddly touched by these very private moments shared with us; once more we felt like the intruders we virtually are, studying the lives of people most of us have never spoken to or met. Paradoxically, we also suddenly felt even more part of a world that we had mostly only known from files and books, and photos, as well as footage of Bundy in court or on mug shots.

We had so often been deliberating amongst ourselves whether all that Bundy could have possibly experienced emotionally he had saved for the two Kloepfer women. Molly's admissions completely shattered the idea of Bundy having had just one shred of un-self-serving humaneness and decency inside him, and personally, I thank both Kloepfer women for giving us this gift of removing all doubt and changing the narrative once and for all.

Molly's words had informed us about how little we still knew, despite our years of immersing ourselves in the case. It was a humbling experience.

One person who read my original Molly article was critical of my not having examined the story the way I had other unconfirmed survivors, bit by bit, piece by piece, weighing their words against Bundy case facts and myths.

Obviously, police files, studying the schematics of Bundy's 1968 VW Beetle and credit card receipts are not going to be of any help in this instance. We simply have no substantial evidence to go on.

When attempting to verify Molly's story, we must predominantly take a closer look at Bundy's interpersonal relationships, and whether the carefully crafted mask he wore in public ever slipped and his entity-self bled into his private life. It did, on many occasions.

Before I list these examples, I would first like to address the accusation towards the Kloepfer women that their intention to republish, consult on Joe Berlinger's "*Extremely Wicked*" movie and be interviewed for Trish Wood's amazon Prime documentary "*Falling For A Killer*" was a) a cash grab and b), quote, "*whoring themselves out for attention.*"

First of all, I have yet to hear the same people suggest that Ann Rule, Richard Larsen or George Dekle sought nothing but attention with their publications. It is known that while each had a part in the Bundy saga, at least Rule at times drastically overstated her relationship with the killer. If we go by these standards, then we may add the unconfirmed survivors' books, pamphlets, blogs and television interviews to the list of people who solely sought to profit from recounting their Bundy stories as well.

Secondly, Elizabeth Kloepfer did not learn of Joe Berlinger's movie project until she stumbled across mentions of it on the internet. Berlinger had been comfortable enough to affirm that his film was going to be made from Kloepfer's perspective. That alone is curious, because he was missing the key ingredient for it in order to accurately do so: Elizabeth Kloepfer.

Berlinger did not see fit to even contact her before revealing he had already started the project. Although he wasn't legally obligated to inform Koepfer of his intentions, doing so would have been the ethical choice to make.

Instead, Berlinger seems to have considered the opinions presented in "*The Phantom Prince*" timeless enough to base "*Extremely Wicked*" on it, a book written nearly 40 years earlier. Did he not anticipate that Kloepfer's opinions on Bundy and interpretation of events between them had likely matured, and changed?

Berlinger forced Kloepfer's hand; she could either sit idly by, watching a stranger earn a considerable amount of money with his personal interpretation of her life experiences, or she could offer to consult on the movie in order to at least try and impact the narrative. Had the film not falsified events as drastically as it did, leaving out Bundy's permanent abuse of Kloepfer entirely, the latter may not have felt compelled to re-publish her book, with additional chapters to clarify her – present and valid – feelings about Bundy, at all. Lastly, Molly did not write her own book but added one chapter to her mother's existing book. Whatever – certain large – sums of money Molly could have made with a memoir of her own, she chose not to.

  ?

Molly Kloepfer	Kimberly Leach	Lynnette Culver	Leslie Parmenter	Susan Curtis	Unidentified Idaho Hitchhiker	Nancy Wilcox	Laura Aime	Melissa Smith	Debra Kent
	12	12	14	15	15	16	17	17	17

To finally delve into the subject at hand: Could Ted Bundy have sexually abused a child? Yes. That is certain because his victims include at least eight minors, their ages ranging from 12-17 years, and because he in part made high schools and high school hangouts his hunting ground.

And after the airing of the documentary centered around Dr. Dorothy Otnow-Lewis, "*Crazy, Not Insane*," we learned that Bundy had also molested at least one of his two sisters while he was a teenager.

In case of Molly, we must now determine: Was Ted Bundy a *pedophile* in the clinical sense however? The DSM-5 diagnosis 302.2 (F65.4), *Pedophilic Disorder*, entails three criteria to qualify for this affliction:

- "An individual who has had arousing fantasies about, urges for, or behaviors with a prepubescent child or children.

- The individual has acted out these sexual desires, or is experiencing significant distress or difficulty as a result of these desires.

- The Individual is 16 years of age, and at least five years older than the child or children […]

    The six specifiers for the disorder are:

- Exclusive type- sexual attraction to children only.

- Non-exclusive type- sexual attraction to adults and children.

- Attraction to boys.

86

- Attraction to girls.

- Incestuous only. (American Psychiatric Association, 2013)."

We cannot say with absolute certainty that Bundy habitually fantasized about prepubescent children, or that he abused other prepubescent and pubescent minors other than Molly and his sister(s).
We can however determine that he appears to have fantasized about teenaged girls, and that on at least two to three occasion he may be considered to have acted incestuously since he was practically a father to Molly for the better of nine years. That alone is not enough for a diagnosis, and so we must seek answers in other behaviorisms of Bundy's:

Detective Jerry Thompson uncovered a collection of Cheerleader magazines in Bundy's Utah apartment. Cheerleading has a long, sordid and surprisingly political tradition in the USA, reaching as far back as the late 1800's and increasingly gaining popularity in the 1940's-60's.
These magazines featured stories and photos of both professional – adult – and high school cheerleading teams. The uniforms are generally revealing and accentuate the female form, or in case of the underage cheerleaders, they accentuate the athletes' un(der)developed child-like bodies.
Perusing several issues of 70's Cheerleader magazines, I noticed that some of the photographs depicted cheerleaders of all ages in poses with an obvious sexual undertone: Legs widely spread, posing cross-legged with the short skirts hiked up their thighs and revealing a glimpse between their legs, sitting atop the shoulders of male team mates, hands on the ground and buttocks in the air while smiling up into the camera.
Many of the cheerleaders wore makeup that are more conventional for adults to wear. Tryouts are tough, one needs not only be an excellent athlete but possess a pleasant physical appearance.
On the other hand, no regular pornography was ever found at Bundy's abodes in Washington and Utah. He himself spoke about how violent pornography had influenced his crimes in his final interview with Reverend James Dobson on January 23, 1989, and yet, that admission is not correct.
Bundy had not had a fondness for violent pornography but for material he used pornographically, which is a world of a difference. Among it were True Detective magazines whose covers usually depicted scantily clad women in distress, their limbs

dramatically spread apart – similarly to those on Cheerleader magazine covers – and their hands bound, mouths open in a silent scream, the latter component equally reminding of "darkside" cheerleader photography.

Both types of magazines sexualized females, and the True Detective magazines stylized them as victims of potent men, men not afraid to "take what they wanted," the caveman approach to intimate relationships.

Bundy's preference for True Detective magazines developed in his early years when he discovered them around the Cowell household. He had witnessed his grandfather treat his wife and the Cowell women aggressively, possibly manifesting in him the belief that love/intimacy and violence/control were inseparable. What is more, his puberty and sexual awakening was informed by said True Detective magazines.

One key ingredient of this unfortunate recipe for disaster is the fact that Bundy admitted to not dating as a teenager because he was too shy, "did not know what made humans want to be friends." Instead he fantasized about fellow classmates he was attracted to. He imagined them in peril, coming to their aid to rescue them at first, essentially playing God.

Later he spun tales of putting the girls in danger himself, yet still being gracious enough to rescue them. But by endangering them, the first step had been made to being a perpetrator, if only in mind. He played not only God the sustainer anymore, but developed into an Old Testament kind of God; one who put his "subjects" in peril to test their love, as God had once done with Job.

Eventually, the fantasies evolved even further, they changed to exclude rescuing the girls, now he was only harming them, and deriving pleasure from it. He had fully slipped into the role of the attackers he had seen on the covers of the True Crime Detectives he so enjoyed.

Bundy's entire emotional development remained stunted throughout his life, with journalists, ex-girlfriends, psychologists and attorneys noting that he appeared like a twelve-year old boy in the body of an adult male.

Most human beings indulge in a form of sexual nostalgia: Our first love, first intimate encounter and the time period during which we discovered our sexuality usually vastly influence our later choice of partner and sexual preferences.

With these two factors in mind, and combining it with the statement that Bundy was a "twelve year old boy in an adult man's body," it would not surprise had Bundy retained a fondness for underage females, more specifically pubescent girls.

This would qualify him as being a *hebephile*, someone attracted to minors between the ages of ~12-14, as well as an *ephebophile*, someone attracted to the age group ~15-17.

Because he was clearly also attracted to adult women as both girlfriends and victims, he may have been a "sexual omnivore," a predator who doesn't discriminate based on age, so possibly also being attracted to females younger than 12.

If that holds true, one explanation for him maybe not having abused any other children might be due to not having had the opportunity to be alone with them. The neighborhood girls, Molly's playmates, he likely only had access to when Molly, Elizabeth Kloepfer, a group of children or the children's parents were present.

So the abuse of Molly may also have been isolated incidents, not related to an attraction to that age bracket but rather because she was available.

Occasional or one-time child molesters may exploit a minor because they experience general arousal, so they opt for quick gratification, not because they were inherently attracted to children but – to put it in blunt terms – "a (female) body was present." None of this mitigates what he did by the way.

In short, while we can neither conclusively prove nor dismiss Molly's allegations, Bundy's murder-rapes of the minors on the photo above and the confirmation about his sister's abuse lend credibility to Molly's claim, as much as the fact that she, having been raised by the man, was among those who knew him most intimately.

She is not less credible, as some insist, because she told her story only now. In fact, in her specific case her testimony is more credible because it surfaced only just now, because she owed us no explanation, she sought no attention, no fame, did not publish her own book, and certainly may not have added her survivor story to the second edition of "*The Phantom Prince*," had it not been for Berlinger repugnantly mythologizing and romanticizing in his movie what life with Ted Bundy was like for the Kloepfer women. Analyzing the tactic Bundy availed himself of when forcing himself on Molly, it is a "classic" among child molesters and groomers.

Those engaging in pedophile activities often try to find a way to have their target accidentally "discover" or otherwise get in visual or physical contact with their genitals. The warm-up phase may include displaying their genitals to the child or in turn, finding ways of grooming the child into showing themselves naked to the adult. Showing may then turn into touching the child, rubbing themselves against the child, eventually until climax, both of which appear happened to Molly.

Molly recounts the uncomfortable ways in which Bundy held her, steadying his grip on her by placing a hand between her legs. When her mother discovered this, she was visibly shaken and forbade him to ever touch Molly in this manner again.

The most chilling accounts included Bundy waiting for Molly in the dark, stark naked, and "playing a game with her," which resulted in him showing her his erection. After which he climbed into bed with her in order to read her a bedtime story, a ruse used to abuse Molly, ending with him ejaculating on the child.

And still, there were those insisting that – just as Molly had cried out in her childish innocence – Bundy had merely accidentally urinated on the child. It appears the human mind, not osmium, is the densest material on planet earth…

After this incident, the sexual abuse came to an abrupt halt it appears. That is, if Molly did not choose not to share with us other such incidents.

This gave those doubting Molly further reason to believe she had fabricated the above events because they expected her to lay out all of her personal vulnerabilities for us, preferably in chronological order. A utopic demand.

Another reason for Bundy to cease his attacks may be ascribed to the growing realization that eventually, Molly might "tell" on him.

What is certain is that Bundy began killing around the time he stopped molesting Molly. He may just have found a fare more potent way to live out his God complex.

And in order not to have anyone have to speculate: I blame Molly in no way for Bundy having murdered countless women and girls, and neither do I blame her mother nor Bundy's first serious girlfriend Diane Edwards.

Molly's personal testimony also included events in which Bundy had been physically abusive.

While playing with her, he had purposefully hurled a ball at her face, deriving pleasure from her shock and pain.

Moreover, he had watched on as she almost drowned, rowing his boat further away from the tired child whenever she came close to pulling herself up at its rim.

The question aside whether Bundy would have bothered saving Molly from drowning had Kloepfer not been at the shore observing the cruel game, all above anecdotes call into question one thing many of us had believed integral to understanding Bundy, that he was not a sadistic killer or personality.

We had believed his words about aiming for a quick, painless kill, and that his victims were usually unconscious due to brain trauma while he was raping and strangling them to death.

The cases of Kathy Parks and Julie Cunningham speak a different language. He prolonged their emotional agony for hours.

Was George Hawkins dead during the entire 4-5 hours he spent with her up on Taylor Mountain?

Did he deliberately choose the anniversary of Kimberly Leach's murder as his wedding date with Carole Ann Boone?

Was naming his daughter Rose an insidious way to increase Eleanor *Rose* Naslund's inner torment, who was, after all, known to incomparably suffer in public, as her interviews go to show?

These events may very well point to Bundy having been profoundly sadistic. When he did not have the opportunity to engage in murder, he held himself over with other thrill-seeking behavior such as theft, womanizing/triangulation, or gaslighting Ms. Kloepfer and his side girlfriends.

In his book *"Violent Mind: The 1976 Psychological Assessment of Ted Bundy,"* Dr. Al Carlisle recounted a story that Larry Voschall had relayed to him in one of their phone conversations.

Two years earlier, Voschall had gone rafting with Bundy and a young woman named Becky Gibbs, observing frightening and drastic personalities changes in his friend. At one point Gibbs had climbed into an inner tube tied to the raft and Bundy undid her halter top and let it fall away, which was greatly distressing to Gibbs. Voschall continued,

"But more than that, we got in a couple of really tight situations which were very unpleasant. He put his head under a waterfall and almost overturned the raft. Becky almost went under. He just seemed to enjoy seeing people frightened. As the trip progressed we went over a waterfall." [At one point Ted let Becky drift in the inner tube over to the waterfall knowing she couldn't swim.]"

This incident is reminiscent of Molly's above anecdote, but also of this morsel of information from Elizabeth Kloepfer's memoir:

Bundy had come within inches of murdering her when he had taken her on a rafting trip one weekend. He had pushed her into the freezing ripples of Yakima River without warning, and strained to keep her head underwater.

Kloepfer remembered that he had not seemed like the Ted she knew, rather, he had seemed as if in a trance. When he finally came out of it and let her go, he gaslighted the terrified woman by insinuating she did not know how to take a joke.

These occasions when Bundy spaced out were already noted by family members.

Another attempt on Kloepfer's life was made while she was asleep one night. Closing all the windows before backing up the fireplace, Bundy had left Kloepfer's apartment in the hope she (and possibly Molly) would suffocate to death.

Bundy did not rape Elizabeth Kloepfer, yet we know from her autobiography, case files, and relevant literature that he was abusive towards her, including sexually abusive. When presenting her with the popular 1972 book "*The Joy of Sex*" by Alex Comfort, Bundy asked to try several practices Kloepfer was not comfortable with but ultimately relented to.

He obliged, or seemingly so, when she did not want to repeat some of the more painful practices, but throttled her against her will while they were being intimate and asked her to play dead on at least one occasion.

One night she awoke to find him peering at her naked body under the sheets with a flashlight, an incident bearing obvious necrophile connotations.

Bundy side girlfriends such as Cathy Swindler – incidentally Seattle Detective Herb Swindler's daughter – and Sandi Gwynn attested to him strangling them during their intimate encounters against their wishes, frightening them and prompting them to withdraw from contact with Bundy.

And just as Bundy acted physically violent towards Molly, he did so with Kloepfer on at least one occasion. Bountiful/Utah Detective Ira Beal recorded on September 17, 1975 that Bundy had hit Kloepfer in the face during a verbal altercation.

In conclusion, Bundy was not only emotionally, physically and sexually abusive – and sadistic – towards his victims but also towards various females in his life.

To think that Bundy would torment adult women and – as it pertains to his victims - minors from age twelve onward, yet not a child in his care, the most convenient and vulnerable target that he could easily groom and control, is highly illogical in my view.

But, to my surprise, even some of those who were leaning towards trusting Molly's tale found something to criticize.

A few of them prefaced their statements by divulging to us they themselves had survived sexual child abuse, proceeding to suggest that Molly had been fortunate because Bundy had at least not killed her.

In other words we were now not only at the stage of comparing pain but also at the stage where fellow survivors criticized their peers for not having been murdered in the process.

Several others argued that Bundy had tried to act decently by covering his erection, suggesting Molly had made a mistake when attempting to pry away his hands in her childish naivety and curiosity.

The question why a grown man in his mid-twenties would remove his clothes to ambush a small girl in the dark, but only after the mother had left the home, did not seem to enter their minds.

As days went by after Molly's chapter was leaked online, the accusations towards the Kloepfers grew more sinister still. – Some went as far as drawing a parallel between Molly's alleged *"abuse ruse"* (as they incorrectly applied the label) and one particular Elizabeth Kloepfer quote from the trailer of the then upcoming *Amazon Prime* documentary *"Ted Bundy: Falling For A Killer,"* in which she had commented that hopefully these episodes would be the end of all things Ted Bundy.

These particular group of doubters believed that Kloepfer's words were indicative of Molly having attempted to deal a fatal blow to the killer's infamy with her fabrication, that she was envious of not having received similar attention throughout her life.

Of course, that makes little sense because there is not a single person among Bundy students who hadn't hoped for the Kloepfers to speak out. Authors, journalists, documentarians, bloggers and others had contacted them both and they had declined, which naturally was their right to do.

It was even suggested that Molly forced herself on Bundy, that she *"wasn't really a child at that age anyway,"* followed by this particular commenter's bragging of her own "voluntary" sexual encounters and formation of a drug habit at age twelve.

It matters little how old Molly was but she was in fact not twelve but far younger, by age twelve her quasi stepfather had already been incarcerated and was preparing to be tried for the murder of another twelve year old child – Kimberly Dianne Leach.

Ultimately, the question was raised why Molly had not immediately told her mother about the abuse, ironically from people who are known to vehemently defend Rhonda Stapley, the woman who had been watching on as young women disappeared around Salt Lake City/Utah, yet did not feel compelled to contact the police to share her knowledge about the offender.

Firstly, we do not know at what point in time Molly admitted to having been abused. Molly wrote about having burnt the last letter Bundy had sent her mother from death row, for fear the latter may be manipulated again, feel guilty for having played a part in his arrest.

It is possible that Molly didn't mention the abuse because of the same reasons, that she did not want her mother to experience any more guilt, shame, embarrassment.

Furthermore, we ought not to discount Elizabeth Kloepfer's age and spiritual history. Kloepfer was born at a time when "personal failures" were viewed as ethically criminal by society.

With her background as a Latter Day Saint, it adds to the possible reasons neither of them made the sexual abuse public before now.

Kloepfer's lack of response to Molly's story in the autobiography does not mean she disbelieves her daughter. She did, after all, add the chapter to the second edition. All it may mean is that Kloepfer did not want to insert herself into a story that she had indeed not been a part of due to not knowing about the abuse. She gave her daughter the leeway to find her own voice and words, and to use her chapter as a self-devised therapeutic tool.

Some researchers cited the woman who had sought to discredit survivor Carol DaRonch in court, Dr. Elizabeth Loftus.
Her lifelong mission is to educate people on the fact that memories change over time, and why eyewitnesses testimonies are not reliable. That is correct, as we have also seen in the case of Carol DaRonch who had remembered that Bundy showed her a police badge, but conflated the image with the one a detective had shown her at the police station.
In other words, while we can experience memory gaps, or fill in these gaps with incorrect knowledge, we cannot fabricate entire events – and believe that they are rooted in reality – unless there is a severe mental disorder at play.
From her writing and interviews on Trish Wood's amazon Prime documentary "*Ted Bundy: Falling For A Killer,*" there is no reason to believe that Molly experiences any such disorder or *False Memory Syndrome*.
Molly was raised by a serial killer, the attention was always hers – and her mother's – had they chosen to accept it.
The second edition of "The Phantom Prince" and the documentary would have sold well simply because the Kloepfers appeared in it.
So what motive could she viably have to intentionally embellish any of her stories to this extent? None.

Molly has also been criticized for admitting that she struggled with alcohol and drug abuse when younger, prompting a handful of people to suggest that they may have addled her brain in such a way that she could not "distinguish fantasy from reality" anymore.
There are several terms attached to memory loss due to alcoholism. Most laymen have heard about blackouts; additionally there are *Korsakoff Syndrome*, Alcohol Amnestic Disorder.
This includes the loss of memories that were already made, the inability to form new memories and loss of ability to learn new information (and skills).
Molly addressed several memories also confirmed by her mother in the book, wrote about memories she had formed as a young-, new- and older adult. And she's successfully worked as a massage therapist in the wider Seattle area.

All of this is yet more circumstantial evidence that those who seek to discredit Molly are grasping at straws.

In fact, Molly's admission to having struggled with substance abuse, and acting out when younger, make her far more believable to me than any other unconfirmed survivor. Both Kloepfer women did not spare themselves at all, at times making themselves look dependent, cantankerous, embarrassing. None of that makes for a recipe for success or being viewed solely favorably.

It appears that Bundy students often grapple with accepting new information on Bundy because we had – over many decades – gotten used to accepting his own personal accounts regarding his childhood, development of the Entity and whom or why he murdered. In other words, he starkly controlled the narrative and how we view him for one.

And secondly he left us with nothing but our own speculations in relation to cases he refused to speak about, which usually involve the cases of underage victims, and his allegedly "normal, near-perfect Christian upbringing" by grandfather Samuel Cowell.

The various ways in which Molly was denied survivor status by the community reminds of her being disallowed to join self-help groups for survivors of violent crime because, as she wrote, the organizers were concerned that her presence might "upset people."
That is reminiscent of male rape survivors who are also mostly denied entry to such groups to heal from their trauma. Just as male survivors are being viewed with suspicion, as if they might snap any second and attack the entire group, Molly was met with the same unfounded suspicion. Where, I ask, is one permitted to turn if one was raised by a sexually sadistic serial murderer then?

One commenter wrote, that the sexual abuse had happened *only one time,"* (which is incorrect as the chapter proves, and which now the documentary "Crazy, Not Insane" also lays out) and she could not believe that anyone would just forget *"how much he cared about [the Kloepfers]."*
Bundy's absence in the days after the incident was, to this young woman alternating between two social media accounts while posting, indicative of remorse.

I wonder how she would have felt about such a statement, had one of her siblings, close friends or even she herself experienced such a crime "only once."
Or if she has ever taken the time to familiarize herself with the devastating effects of child sexual abuse, no matter how often, at what age it happened, regardless of coercion or violence having played a part.

I just don't like the outcome of this news .. people are now saying .. oh ted is a pedo and all of that !!! .. it happened one time ! .. and he didn't come back for days .. he wasn't in the right mind .. and now people are forgetting how much he cared about them just because of this one incident

Like 5d   3

He cared about molly !!! .. it happend when he wasn't in control and it never happened again !!!!! People are making it so much bigger then it actually is

I wish most of all that she, and others who share her opinion, may one day make a concerted effort to not only read up on this subject but spend a few weeks or months, or longer, in survivor groups to understand that sexual abuse is a life-altering and psychologically irreversible event.

Its long-term consequences often entail substance abuse, depression, anxiety, post-traumatic stress disorder, obsessive-compulsive disorder, body dysmorphic disorder and other mental and emotional challenges. In short: All challenges that Molly faced throughout her life.

I previously wrote about *hybristophilia* and its many forms and sub-categories on *CrimePiper* – without judgment, and with the help of several *hybristophiles* as I would like to reiterate. Although the article in question had caused me great grief while I still considered myself part of the Bundy community, when *hybristophiles* were made a target online late last fall due to several articles and interviews painting them all as monsters, I did what I always do with most of any group of people that face a rabid mob. – I put myself in between them and their critics and attackers who wished upon them rape and torture and death at the hands of their object of desire.

I did so, too, because some of my friends self-identify as *hybristophiles*. And while I understand very well that any survivor may find this a horrifying statement, I know these self-identifying *hybristophiles* to be ordinary, decent people with bottomless empathy for the victims, despite having a romantic preference certainly not easy to comprehend or accept for many, even within the True Crime community.

While I want to make clear that many *hybristophiles* I interact with in Bundy-related groups displayed just as much genuine shock and sympathy for the victimized child, I still had to come to terms with the fact that about 30% of the people attacking Molly came from this very camp.

A great disappointment to me, but also to many other *hybristophiles* who vehemently

defended Molly online, losing friends and membership in groups over their stance.
There is a bit more to the reactions of some of these specific *hybristophile* deniers though.
Their denial may very well have stemmed from this:

While somehow they had found a way to stylize Bundy's murderous and non-murderous crimes into the acts of an Easy Rider type of bad boy, child sexual abuse is a bit harder to mythologize. Its denial comes far more easily hence.

A villain is only ever the hero of the other side, and in this instance, Bundy was a character molded into a dark avenger/protector type of character by some *hybristophiles*. Someone who would inflict grievous harm on others but not them, in trade for their love and loyalty.

Others had simply turned the tables on him in their minds. Because he could not prohibit them from having intimate fantasies about him, writing them down or role-playing in relevant groups, they themselves had risen from mere victim to "offender," or thought criminal. They were in full control.

But now that they had found Bundy was very much like their sleazy uncle, older brother or whoever else that had previously harmed them, they had to come to grips with the fact they had virtually chosen to love the embodiment of their own abuser. For years. For decades even.

Moreover, they had to come to grips with never actually having been in control of him, that – even posthumously – he was still very much in control of them, just as their abusers were hence.

That is certainly a very brutal life lie to face, and I say this without irony or any sort of cruel glee but in all sincerity. The only way to protect their mental utopia was to turn reality into a dystopia, by denouncing and attacking Molly.

Eventually, I received one message by someone I had never personally spoken to, accusing me of playing favorites and reminding me that I myself had *"only made a name for myself by shaming raped women."*

A colorful interpretation I won't shy away from addressing in the slightest. And I will do it by asking I would like to ask where Rhonda Stapley's – or any other unconfirmed survivor's – commentary on the updated edition of *"The Phantom Prince"* and *"Molly's Story"* was during that time.

Most of those who had pre-ordered the second edition of *"The Phantom Prince"* received their copy of the book on January 9 and were posting about it far and wide, incidentally the day that Stapley put up one single post on her wall: Another promotion post for her 2016 book. The competition never sleeps after all.

If ever asked about Molly, will she answer similarly as she did on a US morning show in 2016 when compared to Carol DaRonch, insisting that the latter wasn't really a survivor, incomparable to her because DaRonch had "gotten away so quickly?"

Stapley remains among the characters still supported by some, despite the myriad of valid questions her account prompts, yet the same people now oust the Kloepfers? Quo Vadis, Bundy community!

As for the above accusation towards me and what later became the *"Dissection articles"* on *CrimePiper*, I went into investigating all of these cases with no preconceived notion and no agenda whatsoever.

When I was still relatively new to the Bundy case, I did not yet possess the knowledge to adequately determine the likelihood of accounts such as *Snugglehose* seller Rhonda Stapley's and others, and had the patient assistance of seasoned researchers who were kind enough to correct my logical fallacies until I was able to spot inconsistencies on my own.

So to compare Stapley's profoundly flawed story with that of a woman who had been raised by a serial killer over the course of several years is the logic of the lobotomized. While the Kloepfers faced accusations of being money hungry and starved for fame, no one thought to mention that Mrs. Stapley's two *Facebook* profiles are filled with nothing but promotions for her book?

The Kloepfers had not spoken out for decades despite frequent contact and interview requests. How money hungry could they virtually be?

The investigators have done theirs to enlighten the world about the case from their professional viewpoint. Bundy's college professors, childhood-, church-friends and classmates were interviewed, and some authors spent years traveling the "Bundy route" in preparation of their books.

Everyone, even the unconfirmed victims, were heard. We had all been speculating, theorizing and wondering what else there might be. Well. We do not have to wonder anymore. We have our answer now. Bundy was not only a rapist, necrophile, decapitator, mutilator, murderer, stalker, kleptomaniac, pathological liar and cheater, *hebephile/ephebophile*/possible *pedophile*. But the latter part is the one unbelievable component of the story somehow?!

Assorted Stories

After Ann Rule had published *"The Stranger Beside Me,"* hundreds of women contacted her with alleged Ted Bundy survival stories. She made a conceited effort at selecting those she deemed credible to appear in her book, but also responded to those whose stories she could neither verify nor believe occurred.

Nowadays, in the age of the internet, every alleged encounter is printed, told by the unconfirmed survivors, often repeatedly.

I have somewhat grappled with how to present some of these stories in this publication, and ultimately decided that I would only share the names of those who had voluntarily opened themselves up to scrutiny by publicly sharing their stories on *YouTube* channels, their webpages, on television or in their memoirs. I will keep the names of individuals who reported their alleged encounters with the serial killer in *Facebook* groups or on their personal social media accounts private, so as to prevent harassment of them. I have added an asterisk (*) after every name I changed.

*

Ron Oberst-W. (*), who possesses at least two *Facebook* accounts with which he applied to join The Ted Bundy Research Group, had this to say:

"When I was 6 in Colorado Springs, I met him while I was walking to a cemetery. I walked between a victim and him [on] 23rd street. I am writing a book about the man, the evidence points to [him having been] a hitman for the mob/the kids of political rivals."

Mr. Oberst-W.has not responded to inquiries about how he reached the unverified personal gnosis that Ted Bundy was a government-approved assassin.

*

A person named Renée Worth (*) also applied to join several Bundy *Facebook* groups I helped manage. The woman, who has made public that she suffers from hypothyroidism, also writes about her alleged childhood with Bundy, insinuating that local government officials, law enforcement and politicians knew of, condoned and partook in the abuse of her.

R▮▮▮▮▮▮▮▮▮▮▮

August 11, 2019 · ⊙

Recap: I was victim to murder, child porn, forced prostitution.
Abuse was by: judges, attorneys, cops, businessmen, oil men, politicians and
entertainers.
I am a ted bundy Survivor.
I am an informant by choice for the safety of my daughter and myself.
Judge ▮▮▮▮▮▮ is an idiot.
The End

⊙ 2

👍 Like   💬 Comment   ➢ Share

*

In the *BuzzFeed* video, *"Was My Mom Followed By Ted Bundy,"* uploaded to *YouTube* on March 3, 2019, a young man identified as Chris claims his mother was *"followed by a murderer."* As of November 2020, the video had received over 4 million views and 320k likes.

On one occasion in the 70's, his mother and her friends went to Oak Creek Canyon Park, located in the middle of Coconima National Forest in Northern Arizona.

They parked their car in a parking lot after noticing that this place was "almost too open," which, I surmise, is his way of conveying it was isolated.

Chris goes on to admit that his mother had been to the park before, which begs the question why she only just then noticed it was *"too open."*

After a short while, Chris' mother allegedly noticed a man right across the pond they were sitting at. Minutes went by and yet the man was still watching them, *"rubbing his chin thoughtfully,"* as though to convey, *"I see you."*

His mother's first thought was how odd it was that he was out there all by himself. Which is curious as he had just stated it was unusual for the park to be so empty, particularly on a day as nice as that one. One would assume that even in Arizona it's socially acceptable to be out and about by oneself.

Chris' mother noticed how well dressed the man was, thinking to herself that their group of friends should move to another area as she began to grow scared for some reason that is never explained in the clip.

Now, when Chris' mother mentioned this to her sister and friends, they told her that she was overthinking it, being *"crazy."*

At some point the man started walking away at the edge of the pond, *"towards their direction."* Chris continues, *"The scariest part, he was walking with intention."* And how dare he. As if an unaccompanied man at a national park wasn't terrifying enough to encounter for a group of people, he now moved with…intention! However this was determined remains unclear.

Finally, the others agreed with Chris' mother that something wasn't quite right with the situation, deciding to head back to the car in the parking lot. Chris' mother continually cast glances back at their pursuer, and indeed, he followed them, beginning to walk at a faster pace than before.

The group made it back to the car and sped out of there on the same road they drove in on, yet the man was nowhere to be seen.

When the driver, Chris' aunt, looked into the rearview mirror, she pointed out that the man was following them. For this to have happened, the pursuing car must have been awfully close though, which casts some doubt upon how someone can be "gone" one moment and then so close that the group could make out the man's face in the pursuing vehicle.

Chris, now caught in the moment, enhances this truly gruesome story further by claiming that the *"energy in the car felt cold,"* then states that his mother turned around one last time, spotting the "yellowish, cream-colored Volkswagen Beetle" just coming out of the same parking lot. In light of his earlier statements, none of this makes much sense of course. Chris however assures his viewers, *"All my mom knew was, this person is evil. She could feel it."*

The group of three managed to maintain a somewhat safe distance between themselves and the Bug, eventually pulling into a gas station, and watching with relief as the other car passed them.

Whether the well-dressed man from the pond was actually behind the wheel, or whether he, or whoever drove the car, wouldn't have driven past the group without them seeking shelter at a gas station, is unclear.

About fifteen years later, Chris' mother recognized Ted Bundy as their harrowing pursuer when news of his execution were being shown on TV. There, she learned that *"he was well dressed, drove a yellow cream-colored Volkswagen Beetle, and he committed several murders in Colorado. Which is right above Arizona."*

As she continued watching the news segment, Chris' mother received a call by her sister. Without greeting her, she asked, *"Do you think it was him?"* Because sisterly intuition surely will have told her that her sister was just watching the same broadcast on television.

Chris' mother replied, "*I **know** it was him.*"

What *we* know is this: Bundy was a restless driver, who didn't shy away from driving 6-7 hours from Salt Lake City/Utah to the wider Aspen area in Colorado to murder three young women.

A drive from the Aspen area to Coconino County, Flagstaff, would have taken an additional 8 ½ hours however. Is it possible Bundy took time to drive that far? Yes. Is it likely? That is another question.

Here's another good question: What serial killer would go on the prowl dressed "incredibly well?" How could the group even make out that he was dressed well, likely to mean expensive or formal clothing, from a distance, across a pond? Bundy himself wore dark and inconspicuous clothes when going on the prowl, save for one instance at Lake Sammamish when he was spotted in tennis garb. He had coveralls in his trunk at all times. I have some trouble imagining that Bundy, dressed in a suit and tie, would chase after a group of women.

*

Kristee Vetter is a young woman hosting a lifestyle, beauty and shopping vlog on *YouTube*. One of her videos, uploaded to the platform on May 17, 2019, is titled "[M]y *mom's encounter with Ted Bundy*."

Once Vetter's mother actually receives the chance to speak after approximately seven minutes, though never uninterrupted for very long, the viewer learns that Vetter's mother believes to have encountered the man in Bellevue/Washington – after his prison escape. Of course, this is the first crucial mistake in the video, and there are more to follow.

Vetter's mother states she spent time at her friend Suzie's house, when someone knocked on the door. After Kristee Vetter interrupts her mother, her mother asks, "*Did I answer or did Suzie answer?*" To which her daughter replies, "*You answered. That's the way you told me the story.*"

So Mrs. Vetter isn't even actually certain anymore, asking someone who wasn't even born at the time for help to recall her own Bundy encounter memory.

After finding herself face to face with a young man, Mrs. Vetter states she was "*like a deer in headlights, because I was like, 'Oh my gosh!'*"

Kristee chimes in, "*But you recognized him, is the thing.*" Her mother demurely agrees, seeming uncertain. Her daughter continues, *"The way I remember you telling me is, like, you recognized him but it didn't immediately click who he was. You were just like, 'Something's off.' Or was it immediately like, 'Oh shit, that's Ted Bundy?'"*

Vetter retorts, *"Well, it was immediately like, 'Oh shit, that's Ted Bundy,' but it can't be Ted Bundy, so…"*

There's a cut in the video, it's unclear what exactly was cut out or how much of it. The video continues with Mrs. Vetter recalling that her friend Suzie came up behind her and *"she about died,"* slamming the door in "Bundy's" face after saying, *"Goodbye."*

Vetter's daughter laughs, *"Oh Suzie slammed the door? I thought you slammed the door."* None of the two women appear to know what exactly happened on that day. Kristee once more jumps in to help her mother remember details of the alleged incident, asking whether Bundy had said anything to her. Vetter concedes that he asked for directions, but since she wasn't familiar with the area – despite visiting her friend there – she didn't even understand what he was talking about.

The last four minutes of the video include redundant information, are hence insignificant for the purpose of examining this story further.

Now, Kristee Vetter gained a substantial amount of uninformed, i.e. positive, commentary on this video, but a handful of seasoned Bundy researchers tirelessly presented dates, times and facts to Kristee Vetter and her followers in order to correct her various mistakes. After unidentified "friends" of hers joined in attacking us commenters personally, calling us various unflattering names and suggesting we go procreate with ourselves, Kristee Vetter chose to turn off the comment option, deleting all of our comments (which I yet saved) in the process.

Passenger B 3 hours ago (edited)
The biggest problem with this entire story is of course the fact that when Bundy escaped on June 7, 1977 by jumping out of a window located on the second floor of the Pitkin County Courthouse (library), we know with absolute certainty that he did not manage to get out of Aspen, Colorado but remained in the area for six days until he was apprehended again.
Even if your mother had mixed his first escape up with the second one on December 30, 1977 from the Glenwood Springs jail in Colorado, we can just as well trace Bundy's steps and know he was never at any given time in Washington while on the run either. He went to Chicago and via Ann Arbor made his way to Florida where he lay low for several weeks until the Chi O attacks, culminating in the Leach murder.
So either your mother misremembers the year and/or she only believes that the man looked like Bundy but it wasn't him, or this story is simply a fabrication which I hope it is not as that would be very distasteful and offensive to the five brave and resilient women who did survive this man: Karen Sparks, Carol DaRonch, Karen Chandler, Kathy Kleiner and Cheryl Thomas.
Show less

J.Knight78 19 hours ago

Timeline doesn't make sense. Bundy first escaped from the courthouse in Aspen, Colorado in June 1977. He hid in a cabin in the surrounding mountains, then was recaptured after 6 days. The second escape was from jail in Glenwood Springs, Colorado on Dec. 30, 1977. From Colorado he took a plane to Chicago, train to Michigan, drove to Atlanta, then took a bus to Read more

Sarah Lane 4 hours ago

After this initial arrest, Ted Bundy went back to Washington when he was out on bail. It could have been during that time because his face was in all the papers.

Passenger B 4 hours ago

That is not what the two women in the video state. They state he had escaped from prison. We know that Bundy was first arrested by Highway Patrol Sergeant Bob Hayward in Granger, Utah on August 16, 1975 He was bailed out of jail on August 17 and surveillance of him began.
He returned to Seattle by way of plane on November 27, 1975 - still under surveillance - and returned to Salt Lake City around late January 1976.
Despite the evasion games Bundy attempted to play with police (and sadly including Elizabeth Kloepfer in the process) there is simply no way that he would have been unobserved or without a police tail long enough to have hit up a random woman's abode in Bellevue. The insinuation that he would have taken the risk alone is nonsensical. My earnest recommendation is to look at the - very - complete timeline of anything Bundy-related before making any claims.

In March, 2020, one of the closed Ted Bundy *Facebook* groups gained a new member who shared that she had met the serial killer in 1967.

Sarah Boltman* intimated that she was born and raised in Redwood City*/California. Once she received her driver's license she liked to take extended drives, especially in the hills around Stanford University.

One evening, shortly after finishing their first year at Skyline College, she took her friend

Becky* along, who had *"brown hair, parted in the middle."*

The women drove up into the hills when the car unexpectedly blew a tire. Not knowing how to change a tire, Boltman and her friend exited the vehicle to assess the damage. They remained at the side of the road, hoping someone would come by they could ask for help.

Boltman shared with the group that at some point a *"nice-looking young man"* approached. He introduced himself as Timothy Griffiths* and they struck up a conversation during which Griffiths stated he was a physics* teacher at Skyline* college, where Boltman had also attended classes.

"At some point we finally checked the blown tire. He suggested Becky and I get in his car and he would take us to a gas station or to a house way up on a hill, accessible by a long driveway. We said no and he then suggested he'd help us change the tire.
He open the trunk of the car and then closed it saying there was no jack. I remember being surprised that my parents wouldn't have a jack, but I believed him. He kept suggesting that we get in his car, often enough to make me feel more irritated than uncomfortable."

Griffiths headed to his car, which was parked down the road under a bridge. Boltman followed, though she is of the view that he must have asked her to do so as she would never have volunteered.

He took a jack and crowbar out of the car and the two, still immersed in conversation, returned to Becky. Boltman reports that she felt uncomfortable while in his presence.

Because the jack was too small to successfully lift the car, Griffiths once more insisted the girls get into his car. Ultimately, a family came up the road in their van at this point and the father offered to change the tire instead. Griffiths departed without another word, which Boltman thought was *"very, very rude"* and *"a bit odd after maybe 30-45 minutes of conversation."*

Griffiths had left his jack in her car but taken the crowbar back with him, and Boltman decided the next morning that she would track him down to return the jack to him as well. She called Skyline College but they knew of no instructor named Tim Griffiths. Local law enforcement officers confirmed that the street Griffiths had stated the hotel he was staying in did not exist either.

She writes,

"Over the years I learned about Bundy. Once I saw his picture, I KNEW Ted and "Tim" were the same. Years went by and my interest grew in Ted Bundy. I realized if I could prove Ted had owned/borrowed (which he often did) a tan/light brown late model Corvair, that would cinch it."

[...] I know that once while being filmed, his interviewer listed the states in which Ted killed. Ted turned around and said something akin to "Don't forget California."

The man Becky and I met was sophisticated, intelligent, smooth, friendly, and confident. His lying skills were so perfect, his presentation so calm. He was ALREADY an accomplished seasoned killer, that I know in my very being. If I could prove this was Ted, it might open help to up cold case files. Who knows how far this could go... The Zodiac killer was seen driving a tan or brown Corvair too..."

Boltman appears to imply that if it wasn't Ted Bundy who had wanted to abduct her, it could at least have been the Zodiac because of he and "Tim" drove the same model and make vehicle. The Zodiac was described as a middle aged, sturdy man whereas both Bundy and "Tim" were young, slender, handsome.

Several weeks earlier, this story – though not as rich in detail – had been shared in the same group by another member, Carin Pembroke (*).

What does this mean? Perhaps it means that Bundy had attacked two women from the same state in the same year in the same manner, which is a possibility. Another possible explanation could be that this was an alternate account of the same person who had previously shared her story in one of the groups after it had been deleted by administrators.

One of the two women could have also "borrowed" this story from the other. We can't determine what happened here. The only thing we can agree on is that there was never and will never be a shortage of new Bundy stories surfacing.

*

On July 5, 2015 Susanne Crawford published her article *"3 Close Calls With Ted Bundy"* for the *Spectrum* website – including her account it's actually four close calls.

While on her way to exit Brigham Young University in early August 1975, Susanne Crawford crossed paths with whom she describes as a handsome, curly haired man around thirty years of age. His eyes were green and mesmerizing, and Crawford believes she had "felt" these eyes watching her while she was on a call inside the building.

The man *"placed himself strategically"* between her and the exit and addressed her. *"You*

have such long, beautiful hair," he told Crawford, *"You really are a pretty woman. I love your eyes, they are captivating."* He continued, *"May I walk you to your car?"*
Because she was married, Crawford declined Bundy's offer, telling him that her husband was about to pick her up, which she admits was untrue but seemed the most polite way to blow him off. According to her, Bundy turned on the spot and nearly ran out of the building, leaving her dumbfounded at his quick departure.

This concludes Crawford's Bundy encounter, yet she provides further speculations about his "socially unacceptable" behavior, elaborating on several incorrect Rule-isms such as all of his victims likening his girlfriend Diane Edwards.
Her final musings involve the question whether Bundy's victims ever sensed any danger from him. Because "psychopaths have no conscience, and therefore have no guilt," Crawford believes this may have accounted for why he seemed so normal to her.
Could Crawford have met Bundy? Certainly. The timeline fits, Bundy was in SLC/Utah at the time, his arrest by Bob Hayward occurred approximately two weeks later.
Due to its brevity, there's also nothing in the story we could confirm or debunk.
The one thing that was either inadequately explained or seems like a contradiction is that mere paragraphs earlier, Crawford had implied Bundy had had such an eerie aura about him that she had felt his eyes watching her even before she had actually seen or met him out in the hallway. She had elaborated on how perplexing his immediate departure was after she had not permitted him to walk him to her car. But now he seemed completely normal to her?

*

Susanne Crawford next recounts the story of a woman named Judy Turner. The only information Turner provides is that she lived in West Valley City in summer of 1975 when she met a "handsome man" at what is now the Fred Meyer Store. He said to her, *"You're such a pretty lady, would you like to get some coffee?"* But Judy, much like Crawford, pointed to her wedding ring and the man disappeared without uttering another word. Turner is of the opinion that she fit Bundy's "profile" because she was *"tall, with long dark hair and a thin build."* The man gave her an odd feeling and she recognized him by his eyes when he was arrested around two weeks later.

*

The last story Crawford shares with Spectrum readers is that of Pat Kraft, who is just as eager to inform us that she wore her *"long dark hair parted in the middle,"* and that she,

107

too, "*was tall and thin.*"

She believes to have met Bundy while attending the Sunday evening mass on the University Of Utah campus in 1974. While taking communion, she noticed a "*handsome man*" watching her from the back. He approached her after mass, insisting that she accompany him to his motel room to share some wine with him. Kraft is quoted saying,

"*As he talked to me, I heard a voice say in my head, 'you want me to go with you so that you can kill me.'*"

*

Pam Prine was a freshman at Brigham Young University in Provo/Utah in 1974. While on her way to a sewing class she spotted a "handsome gentleman" in a suit with his eyes glued on her as he watched her enter Wilkinson Center. He asked her, "*Hi, do you go to school here?*" When Prine affirmed this, he took a look at her umbrella and replied, "*I've seen such good people here. I'm from out of town and I need to go downtown Provo to speak. Could you walk me to my car so I don't get my suit stained in this rain?*"

Prine agreed, but when they walked through three different sections of the parking lot that took them farther and farther from Wilkinson Center, she eventually asked him where he'd parked his car. His reply was vague.

Suddenly, he gripped the back of her belt but Prine tore herself free and ran away, losing her umbrella in the process.

Although she told a friend about it and this person suggested she tell campus security about the incident, she declined, fearing she'd just overreacted.

In 1989, while living in Arizona, she watched

"*a Ted Bundy show starring Mark Harmon. It was the night before Td Bundy was executed. As I watched the movie, I thought it was strange that it said that he was in Provo and had killed a girl there. [...] As I watched the rest of the movie, they showed a picture of Ted Bundy, I looked at that face and saw those yees, and I knew it was him who I ran away [from] at BYU. [...] I looked just like them – Tall, thin, long hair parted in the middle...*"

When discussing these stories with other Bundy historians, many agreed that they seemed likely. I wasn't quite as enthusiastic however, and suggested that one might be inclined to believe them because of their brevity. There are no dramatic overstatements as in some other cases I wrote about in this publication, and after all, we knew that

Bundy had hunted on campuses. It's feasible that Bundy did dry-runs at college campuses, or tried in earnest to kidnap college students but failed, having to settle on high school students instead.

And yet, the lack of just one college aged victim in Utah (and Idaho) speaks volumes. There, he abandoned the injury ruse and very deliberately abducted high schoolers between the ages of 12 and 17.

Likewise, he changed his victimology and modus operandi once more when breeching into Colorado. All this was done in order to avoid that law enforcement agencies would start suspecting they had a cross-country serial offender on the loose. It would have been unwise – and uncharacteristic – of Bundy to take such a risk.

Ted Bundy

Why, this chapter may confuse some, and appall others. Ted Bundy an unconfirmed victim?! Does this not belittle the harm inflicted on others by this man? I'd like to point out that it is not my intention to compare pain or intimate that Ted Bundy's victimhood is comparable to that of the females he murdered.

However, I have reason to suggest that Bundy, too, was a victim of sorts. He was a victim of family members and of his neurodiverse ("abnormal") brain.

Nowadays, it is undisputed that the ingredients for someone to become a serial killer consist of several components. This may include genetic factors, a predisposition to "inherited" psychiatric illnesses, a neurodiversity or head trauma resulting in brain damage. Furthermore a difficult upbringing which may include any type of abuse or neglect, and a vivid fantasy life, paired with (self-)isolation play a part.

Why some of those individuals who were abused early in life become offenders and others refrain from doing harm, is one of the many unsolved questions which we hope neuroscience will in the future be capable of answering.

Mental illness, violence and trauma are usually a generational issue. Abuse is passed down from parent to child, and this cycle is exceedingly difficult to break. To put it in the simplest of terms: Hurt people hurt people.

The Cowell Family

Bundy's grandparents, Samuel F. Knecht Cowell and Eleanor Cowell, had three daughters, Eleanor Louise – Bundy's mother, Julia – named after Samuel's mother, and Audrey.

Samuel, born September 23, 1898 in Chicago, was reported to have been a violent choleric by family members, friends and neighbors alike, who sometimes shouted at someone it seemed only he could see.

This suggests that Cowell either experienced psychotic breaks or may have had an undiagnosed mood and/or delusional disorder.

It also took very little to send him into a flying rage and become verbally as well as physically abusive towards others.

Additionally, he appears to have been obsessed with pornography to the point of letting his magazines and other material he used pornographically openly lie around the house, although his main stash remained in the family's greenhouse.

Even nowadays we would be horrified and consider it child abuse to learn if children were raised in a home where pornography was readily available; but almost a century earlier, Cowell's mere interest in such material was not only considered psychologically and sexually deviant, as well as deeply shameful for the family, but indeed borderline criminal.

Family also remembers Cowell as a proud racist, equally loathing Catholics, African-Americans, Jews and Italians, and frequently engaging in animal cruelty, kicking the family dog on more than one occasion and swinging the neighbor cats by the tail. He also enjoyed to go hunting, and though not definitively corroborated, it has been rumored he did so not for the meat but for the thrill of the kill.

Louise's mother Eleanor Miriam Cowell, neé Longstreet, was born on February 16, 1895 in Philadelphia, Pennsylvania. She also experienced mental health challenges, possibly exacerbated by her marital challenges.

She received electroshock therapy for *Psychotic Depression*, altering between states of crippling depression, agoraphobia, and manic episodes during which she was agitated and aggressively cheerful.

Psychotic Depression was later renamed *Bipolar Disorder*, a mood disorder marked by phases of euphoria and depression. It remains undisclosed whether Eleanor, too, experienced hallucinations, as her husband did. Some with *Bipolar type I* experience hallucinations, as do those with *Bipolar, Schizoaffective type*. *Schizoaffective Disorder* itself is a psychiatric condition characterized by features of schizophrenia and a mood disorder (*Bipolar*).

Bundy's mother Eleanor Louise Cowell was born in Philadelphia, Pennsylvania, on September 21, 1924 and died on December 23, 2012 in Tacoma after a long lasting illness. Louise, a devout churchgoing secretary, found herself unwed yet pregnant at the age of 22, a scandal during that time.

It's unclear whether it was her own decision or whether her parents forced her to have the baby at the *Lund Home For Unwed Mothers*, which was also known as "*Lizzie Lund's Home For Naughty Ladies*" back in the day.

The Home was located in Burlington, Vermont, far enough away so Louise would not have to worry about running into anyone she might know. It's interesting that she did not enter the home prior to September 23rd, 1946, meaning at seven months along she was already very visibly pregnant at that time.

When discussing the matter with a friend from Pennsylvania, she mentioned that someone close to the family had once told her Louise was to have the babe at home, yet when Eleanor was re-committed to a psychosocial hospital, the family was allegedly concerned it could mess with their narrative and timeline of events. It was unclear when Eleanor would return, so to have a new baby in the home would have put the family honor at risk. Though I have no reason to doubt the person who relayed this fact to me, it must be clear this is uncorroborated hearsay only.

However, this offers up another possible explanation why Louise returned to Philadelphia without little Ted. If her mother was still at the hospital, and neighbors may have known about it, how would the nightly cries of a newborn fit into that equation if she was the child's mother?

My friend Eden O'Brien once asked whether it may have been possible that Louise initially left her son at the Lund Home because she did not want to expose him to Samuel's direct or indirect abuse. This then begs the question why she did return to reclaim him a few months later. Several possible scenarios come to mind:

She may have done so out of love for her child, a sense of duty she felt towards her parents, because her family pressed her to do so, or also because she knew what life at the Lund Home and in any other foster home or family would be like for him. At home in Philadelphia she would be able to protect the boy from Samuel, at least on occasion, whereas she would not be able to do the same for him at Lund's. Had he been adopted or given to a foster family, she would also not have had any insight or control over keeping him safe.

What still rouses some people's suspicion is the fact Samuel Cowell reacted quite aggressively whenever the parentage of his grandson was brought up. This has prompted many to suspect that he himself was the father.

We cannot say either way, but considering that the family did admit to Samuel's

fondness of pornography and violence – yet never even only hinted at Bundy stemming from incest – I consider it unlikely. Likewise, in Alex Gibney's 2020 documentary, Dr. Dorothy Otnow Lewis, who assessed Bundy at Raiford Prison (Union Correctional Institution), Florida, stated that Bundy was not Cowell's son. Where she received this information from is unclear, yet it is easily imaginable that both psychologists and investigators have more information on Bundy's background than what they are willing or permitted to make public. Lastly, Cowell's aggressive reaction when faced with questions about Bundy's father is not uncommon for parents who found their family and name "dishonored" by the birth of a "bastard," and do not have to mean that he was the father. But

William Lloyd Marshall

of course the rumors of incest were further facilitated by Louise's making very vague and contradictory statements regarding the child's biological father. At first she insisted that a navy sailor named Jack Worthington had seduced her. Later she claimed the father was a man named Lloyd Marshall.

Aurore Sage remarked on her old Ted Bundy tumblr page that the only man of that name during that time would be a William Lloyd Marshall, a married man aged forty, not aged thirty as Louise had claimed.

The likeness to Bundy on this particular photo is unmistakable. In all fairness, one single – rather grainy – black and white picture is still not enough to reliably determine whether they were related or not.

There have been those who criticized Louise's "decision" to return home after giving birth at Lund's. We should consider the historical and psychological context here.

During the 40's the wage gap between men and women was dramatic, making it nearly impossible for women to support themselves, let alone a child.

Likewise, finding housing as a single mother was almost impossible; hardly any landlord wanted someone so disreputable associated with their name or buildings.

Louise had no other realistic option but to return to her childhood home, and as mentioned above she did so without the boy initially. It was reportedly her father Sam who insisted she return, months later, to collect her son.

Coming from an abusive upbringing, Louise very likely also suffered from what is known as "*trauma bonding*," which is the emotional dependence of an abused individual on her abuser. It develops due to misunderstanding abuse as love and care because an adequate comparative framework of what real love and care entail is missing. *Trauma bonding* is, in short, a form of Stockholm Syndrome. Bundy grew up right in the middle of this, possibly assuming that it was normal for men to abuse women, that in fact to abuse and control women was a way of showing love, and even responsibility.

When Samuel's mood swings and erratic behavior supposedly worsened over the years, the family urged Louise to remove herself and little Ted from the home. This means there's yet another powerful element that contributed to fracturing Bundy's psyche.

For prior to Louise moving to Tacoma in 1950, she had her as well her son's last name changed from Cowell to Nelson. Hence Bundy was not only removed from the only parents he had ever known, having to come to terms with the fact his parents were suddenly his grandparents and whom he had believed to be his sister was his mother, but his name – a large part of a person's identity – was taken away as well. It may have felt like the eradication of his very self to the young child. Was there a sense of having been betrayed by those closest to him, awakening the permanent distrust and isolation he was plagued with as an adult?

Shortly after the move, Bundy's last name was changed again when his mother married a man she'd met at her local Methodist Church, John Culpepper Bundy; thus the confusion continued for little Bundy.

As Kevin Sullivan reaffirmed in *"The Bundy Murders,"* it was then that Bundy learned about his parentage, despite the various rumors involving his teenage cousin John taunting him about being illegitimate, or the allegation that Bundy traveled to Virginia to learn about his origins at eighteen years old.

When Louise married Johnnie, her son was already well aware of his origins. Whether he could comprehend and emotionally process the meaning of all this is another question entirely though.

Bundy & Kloepfer Family Dynamic Parallels
The relationship with his stepfather was a strained one, and Bundy took many an opportunity to demonstrate his superior intellect to good-natured, hard-working, yet less educated Johnnie.

There were only two familial relationships that appeared to matter to Bundy. The one with his brother Richard, fifteen years his junior, whom he babysat and cared for on a daily basis, fulfilling the role of substitute father, in part also due to the age gap. And the one with his mother Louise, whom he remained in regular contact with throughout his life, and who may have become a quasi-partner in his mind, a mother-wife.

I want to make absolutely clear that this is not to insinuate incest or a latent incestuous desire towards his mother but to illustrate subconscious thought patterns, paired with expectations turned into entitlement later in life.

If this theory holds true, Bundy would have considered himself the man of the house. However, he was not, his stepfather was, meaning he was his rival. This could in part explain the continued animosity towards Johnny, and why Bundy never responded well to the attempts of the latter to bond via common activities.

If we go even further back in time and consider that Louise married Johnny in 1951, when Bundy was four years old, something else in regards to child development comes to mind.

We know that most children between the ages of approximately four to six years old often go through a phase during which they wish to marry one of their parents. Again, the underlying theme here isn't incest but an innocent attempt at bonding with the parent of the other sex, of wanting to adopt certain traits of theirs the child admires and wants to develop within themselves.

114

In Bundy's case, we must keep in mind that he had rather recently suffered somewhat of an identity crisis because of the changes of his last name and the loss of the family, and family hierarchy, as he had known it.

When Louise became pregnant shortly after marrying Johnnie, Bundy had more than common sibling rivalry to handle. His entire sense of self had already been annihilated, and now his mother was "being taken from him" via a new infant that extensively depended on her constant attention. This may have prompted Bundy to feel as though he was about to lose the last member of his "real" (blood) family, that he had to fight for her attention and love.

So the only way to re-establish that bond and claim his identity, particularly as more of his siblings were brought into the world, was to assume a place by Louise's side as an equal quasi-partner of hers, and father to his own siblings.

In the Netflix documentary "*Conversations With A Killer: The Ted Bundy Tapes,*" Bundy stated that when he entered a relationship with Elizabeth Kloepfer and became a stepfather for Molly, the idea of being part of a family "*was a whole new dimension to living that I had never seen before.*" This initially curious remark confirms what I wrote about Bundy viewing himself as the odd one out in the Bundy family, in fact he was at all times also the odd one out (the "bastard") in the Cowell family.

When assuming the role of father figure for Molly, there was no rival as there had been with Johnnie. Molly's father lived in a different state and played a minor role in the child's life.

As Kloepfer admitted in her autobiography,

"I handed Ted my life and said, 'Here. Take care of me,' [...] "*He did in a lot of ways, but I became more and more dependent upon him.*"

So it is possible that when Bundy subconsciously realized that he would never have a father (figure) in his life, he became one instead. First for Richard, and later he continued this pattern throughout his romantic relationships. (See also: Utah girlfriend Leslie Knudson and her son's relationship to Bundy.) He became so dominant in relationships that he wasn't a father figure for his partners' children but for his girlfriends too. I am of the mind that he required this dynamic in order to subconsciously reassure himself that he was in control, that there were no uncomfortable surprises (sister-mother/parents-grandparents) coming his way. He expected women to fulfill a certain role not predominantly because he was an emotional tyrant but because of his deep-set insecurity.

Of course, there's more to all of this as Ted Bundy wasn't a noble character by any stretch of the imagination. As mentioned previously, Bundy molested both his sister and Molly. So where would a – likely teenaged – boy get the idea to sexually abuse his own sister? This behavior is learned, not ingrained. I want to drive home the point that child sexual abuse does not create offenders per se, yet it is known that an overwhelming percentage of child molesters state that they themselves were molested as children. Whether one is inclined to believe them is another question that I'm not here to answer.

So, all of this then leads us back to two things, Samuel Cowell and Bundy's later modus operandi as a killer.

As Bundy researchers Joanne Moss and Abigail Hansmeyer once remarked to me, when Bundy abducted his first victim, Linda Ann Healy (conventionally misspelled as Lynda), he made her bed. He tucked in the sheets, and went as far as hanging up her nightgown in the closet. His first and surviving victim Karen Sparks, was left in her bed, but with the duvet covering her body, which is why her roommates believed her to be asleep when they peeked into her room.

This is not just a modus operandi but a ritual, and one that many sexually abused minors are taught, or rather are forced into learning, by their molesters. It serves two functions, the first is to eradicate all possible physical or forensic traces of abuse. The second is to leave a dream-like quality to the abuse: Was it real, did it really happen if there are no traces in my bed, my room, on my clothes and sheets? The child asks itself. This is a form of particularly heinous gaslighting. Although the diagnosis is heavily debated among clinicians, some psychologists and therapists state that this type of sexually motivated gaslighting can create a fracture of the psyche to the degree that the victim develops *Dissociative Identity Disorder* (formerly known as *Multiple Personality Disorder*). The child develops "alters," sometimes starting out with an "abuse alter" that is present during the sexual assault. It is the part or personality (trait) of the child that is "strong" enough to handle the abuse. After the ritual of eradicating every trace of abuse is completed, the core personality re-emerges. Or alternatively, another alter that eases the child back into its core persona.

Now, Sandi Holt is considered by many to be an incomparably weak source of information on all things Bundy. But if we entertain the notion that Bundy was indeed sexually abused by a scout leader as Holt intimated in one of her – many – interviews, his later modus operandi suddenly seems quite easily explicable.

Diagnoses

Bearing in mind his grandparents' mental health experiences and his upbringing,

Bundy's *Bipolar* diagnosis, which he received from Dr. Dorothy Otnow Lewis, is not unanticipated. It is not uncommon that *Antisocial Personality Disorder* is co-morbid with mood disorders such as *Bipolar, Depression,* or even other personality disorders.

Otnow Lewis also attested that Bundy experienced *Dissociative Identity Disorder*. Some believe she solely based this finding on Bundy's statements regarding his "Entity," the part of him intent on engaging in violent criminal actions. Bundy had attempted to explain to Otnow Lewis that his murderous urge appeared almost like a separate entity, one he had conversations with in his head, and that tormented him until he offended again. Only when it was satisfied did it remain quiet for a while. This yet contradicts Bundy's proclamation to FBI agent Bill Hagmaier of "simply having liked killing."

Some have posited that Otnow Lewis overdiagnosed Bundy because *Dissociation* can already be a symptom of *Bipolar Disorder*. The Dissociation comes in two variations, *Depersonalization*, namely detachment from the self, and *Derealization*, which is to mean the detachment from the person's surroundings, so from the real world. *Depersonalization* can lead to the creation of "becoming" a different version of oneself. Slipping into one or several other personalities one mentally created. This is either done consciously, or involuntarily, in which case it's a delusional state.

Bundy's *Bipolar* diagnosis sounds even more solid once we take into consideration the accounts of those many others who witnessed the killer "space out" on occasion.

Bundy's lawyer Polly Nelson, reported in her book, *"Defending The Devil: My Story As Ted Bundy's Last Lawyer,"* that she had repeatedly observed Bundy pacing up and down in his cell, agitatedly muttering to himself and seemingly unaware of his surroundings. Arresting Florida officer David Lee said the same, Bundy seemed incoherent upon his arrest, intelligibly muttered to himself and informed the officer that he wished Lee had killed him.

The trance issue is equally echoed by Elizabeth Kloepfer, as remarked in my earlier chapter about Molly's story and the rafting incident.

Indeed, Bundy appears to have experienced "trance states" even in his younger years. Kevin M. Sullivan mentions such an incident in *"The Bundy Murders."* A teenaged Bundy accompanied a great aunt of his to the train station after dusk, where he dissociated, became strangely distant, and frightened the woman.

On one occasion Bundy's aunt Julia woke up from a nap and found herself surrounded by kitchen knives, the tip of the blades pointing towards her. Standing in front of her was little Bundy, who – in some accounts – had a "dazed look" upon his face, in other accounts he was grinning fiendishly. Dr. Otnow Lewis, who had had contact with Julia Cowell, had once remarked in the Myra McPherson's 1989 *Vanity Fair* article, *"The Roots*

Of Evil" that the story had been embellished over the years. It's a fair question to ask –
would a three year old boy already be acutely aware that knives were considered
"threatening?" And was to frighten his aunt his actual intention. Likewise, was Julia
surrounded by knives only or was emphasis placed upon this specific type of cutlery
after it became known that Ted Bundy was a psychopathic murderer?

Children growing up in a healthy family dynamic have been observed to test out
boundaries and engage in power struggles with family members. Dolls are being
decapitated, property is destroyed or stolen, verbal and physical aggression may occur.
In short, the infamous knives incident may not have held the significance some need it to
have in order to feel safe - as if obscure behavior were a reliable precursor to predict
serial killing.

   Bundy's genetic predisposition, his confusing and abusive childhood experiences, his
self-isolation due to "not knowing what made people want to be friends," led to him
developing strange fantasies. In these fantasies, he was in control, he wouldn't have to
fear rejection.

His exposure to True Detective magazines and his grandfather's pornography collection
appears to have played a role in this unfortunate development, and the creation of his
"Entity."

None of this excuses the sexual abuse of minors, or the murder of dozens of innocent
female adults and children. Each event in his life, each thought process and deed helps
explain his mental and moral decline however.

Witnesses Adding To The Narrative Years Later

Sylvia Meixner, neé Valint, was fifteen years old when she overheard Ted Bundy strike up a conversation with Janice Ann Ott at Lake Sammamish State Park on July 14, 1974. Meixner witnessed Bundy leading Ott away from the lake, thinking nothing more of it until several weeks later, when she watched a television broadcast on the disappearance of Ott and Denise Marie Naslund.

When Ott's photo was shown on TV, Meixner realized that she had witnessed the abduction in process and told her father about it. He immediately took her to the police station to give a witness statement to aid in the solving of the case.

Meixner did an excellent job in describing the details of Bundy's and Ott's interaction, even relaying to investigators parts of the conversations she had overheard. Without her, we would not have known that the killer introduced himself to Ott as "Ted." As one researcher noted, it's often misstated that Bundy introduced himself to various young women at the lake, but as records show that is not the case.

The entirety of Meixner's original statement, which Kevin M. Sullivan also published in his third Bundy book, *"Ted Bundy's Murderous Mysteries: The Many Victims Of America's Most Infamous Serial Killer,"* reads as follows:

"On July 14, 1974, at about 1230 hrs., I was at Lake Sammamish State Park, with Kathy Veres and Pam. We were sitting on the beach close to the water.

A girl I have positively identified as Jan Ott came up near me and she was on a bicycle. She laid her towel down; she had a pair of cut-offs and a shirt that was tied in the front that showed her stomach. The cut-offs were jeans. She had a dark colored knapsack. She took off her cut-offs and shirt and lay down. She had on a black bikini. I think she had leathered colored thongs.

She lay there for about ½ hour. Then a guy came up to her. He is about 5'6" to 5'7", medium-build, blondish-brown hair down to his neck, parted on the side, had dark tan, left arm in sling. The cast started at wrist and bent around the elbow. He had on white tennis shoes, white socks, white shorts, and a white "T" shirt.

He said, "Excuse me, but could you help me put my sailboat onto my car because I can't do it by myself because I broke my arm."

She said, "Well, sit down and let's talk about it. Where's the boat?"

He said, "It's up at my parent's house in Issaquah."

She said, "Oh, really, I live up in Issaquah."

She said, "Well, okay."

She stood up and put on her clothes. She picked up her bike and said, "Under one condition, that I get a ride in the sailboat."

He said, "My car is in the parking lot."

She said words like, "Well, I get to meet your folks then."

He had asked her who she knew in Issaquah.

They left like they were going out to the parking lot. They were only on the beach for about ten minutes.

He had a small English accent, kinda like a fag. He had tiny sideburns. He was smooth talking. He was definitely a white male and could not be mistaken for a Latin or Hawaiian. His clothes looked like he was rich and dressed to go sailing. [Ann.: Bundy wore a tennis outfit during most of the day.]

He stated that his name was Ted, after she said "My name's Jan." I was about two feet from Jan. We were about a hundred yards from the Rainier function. [Ann.: The Mount Rainier Company picnic event.] He walked up from the west."

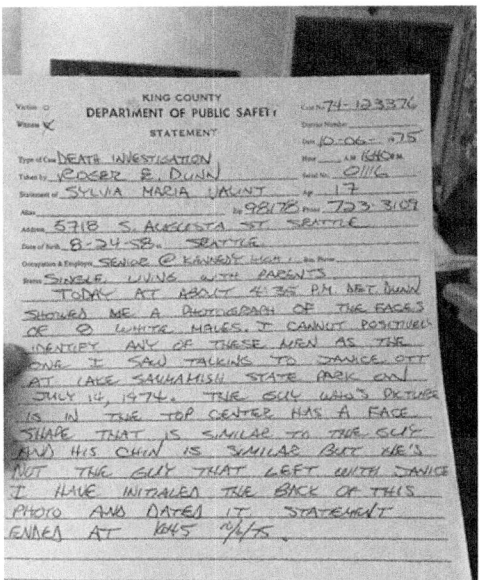

Detective Roger Dunn contacted Meixner again in 1975, and from Kevin M. Sullivan's copy of the report, as depicted above, it's obvious her story remained the same.

In the four part documentary from 2018, *"How It Really Happened,"* Sylvia Meixner was among the guests interviewed about the Lake Sam incident.

Only now she suddenly stated that Bundy had walked up to her in an attempt to convince her to help him with his sailboat. She allegedly refused to aid him and so Bundy moved on to Janice Ott instead.

This contradicts her earlier testimony.

DEA agent Jerry Snyder spent his day off at the beach on July 14, 1974, sitting in close proximity to Meixner. His statement to police equally contradicts Meixner's latest addition to the story. Snyder stated that Bundy walked around, looking over the crowd at the beach, and only stopped to address Ott.

Why do some witnesses dramatically change their story years later? As mentioned earlier, renowned psychologist Dr. Elizabeth Loftus pointed out that humans tend to fill in memory gaps with events or details that appear most plausible to them according to their personal life experiences and expectations of social interactions and rules. It is rare that entire new storylines are created in the process though.

It is a true enigma what compelled Meixner to veer off of her original testimony, and we may only speculate as to why she did so. In recent years, the Bundy market was flooded with many a publication, with movies, documentaries, comic books, novels and more. Each documentary and book strove to present something new and unheard of. We were fortunate to finally hear the Kloepfers speak, Polly Nelson resurfaced, so did several contemporaries of Bundy's, as well as eyewitnesses. I imagine the pressure on the ordinary person to "deliver" to be immense. Whether it is sheer overwhelm that drives some to misspeak, suddenly believe they remember additional details or there are other perks involved are some of the speculations I have heard and read but also pondered myself.

Meixner is of course not the only one to add details that had not even found their way into the official record decades earlier. She is joined by Liz Kloepfer's former close friend MaryLynne Chino who enjoys sharing with anyone and everyone pointing a camera at her how she always knew Bundy to be an unsavory character. And there is our old friend Sandi Holt who some believe "borrowed" an entire event from the case of Keith Jasperson, and his daughter Melissa Moore's autobiography, respectively. Holt shared in the *Investigation Discovery* dumpsterfire documentary *"Ted Bundy: Mind Of A Monster"* – which misrepresented an Edmund Kemper quote as having been uttered by Bundy and spliced together recordings from different Bundy tapes on which he spoke about completely different cases – that Bundy once hung a cat from the clothesline in the backyard, torturing it and watching on as the animal experienced an agonizing death. Of course, there are coincidences aplenty whenever Holt is involved, so who is to say that not both Jesperson and Bundy coincidentally hung a cat from a clothesline, decades apart?

Victim-Players: Possible Motivations

Thanks to those survivors who have helped bring offenders to justice by reporting their attacker to the proper authorities, enduring long hours of questioning, media and police scrutiny, that I remain perplexed whenever I encounter those who tell the most abstruse of supposed Bundy encounters. However, I'm also eager to comprehend the motivations of people who repeatedly perpetuate such obviously flawed, if not outright untrue, tales publicly.

Years ago, Colorado researcher Vince Lahey asked me what anyone would possibly stand to gain from deliberately fabricating an attack on oneself. In the process of this conversation, I was told by several people who were part of the conversation, that we must at all times and without question believe anyone who presents us with such reports.

When I began sharing online that I was examining the unconfirmed survivors, reactions were mixed. Few applauded my pursuit, some removed me from their online study groups or their friends list. I mention this because I observe the decline of a healthy discourse culture with growing concern. Two years ago, I was added to a *Facebook* conversation in which a Los Angeles-born documentary film-maker shared her plans to "destroy" the lives and reputations of anyone and everyone who dared question Rhonda Stapley as well as any other self-reported Bundy victim.

If we research Bundy's crimes, childhood, mental state and family, then we must also research the unconfirmed victims's stories. Just as we give the accused the benefit of a doubt – consider that they may be innocent – we must give the accusers the benefit of a doubt – consider that they may be wrong.

I for one am convinced that it ultimately serves actual survivors better if law enforcement and psychologists ask all the right and all the hard questions, as re-traumatizing as it undoubtedly is to those who were victimized. I say this as someone who survived crime and experienced the devastating effects of crime on family members of mine. In my mind what holds true for law enforcement and psychologists also holds true for True Crime researchers, writers, bloggers, documentarians. We must apply the same investigative rigor as the authorities do if we want to understand the Bundy case in its entirety.

Some stand firm in their belief that we need not probe further into an unconfirmed victim's account because they cite dubious statistics that have shown only 3% of all rape stories to be untrue. These alleged 3% were uncovered because these individuals were properly probed and investigated, however.

Those men and women who were determined to be innocent of a sex crime often continue to be shunned by family, friends and co-workers. They struggle to find employment, housing, they may even have to uproot their entire lives, move to a different city or state, in order to rebuild their lives. Every single person who is affected by these 3% is a true and real victim that suffered through the terrible trauma of being accused of a grievous offense.

In the case of Ted Bundy, there is no doubt that he was a rapist and murderer. Yet accrediting more attacks to him that he did not actually perpetrate, solely because he was a prominent serial killer, is morally bankrupt in my view. It makes a mockery out of his real victims and all real survivors. To portray yourself as a victim in light of what Bundy's 30+ victims lived through, strangulation, brutal rapes, emotional torment, brain damage, dismemberment, decapitation, surgeries, nightmares, PTSD, indicates a complete lack of comprehension of the gravity of these crimes, as well as a concerning lack of empathy towards them. Additionally it may falsify the timeline of events and distorts our knowledge of the psychopathology of the offender.

Fabricators miss crucial details in their stories. They exclusively write from a mental standpoint, not an emotional one because they're not reliving an actual event. They once imagined a complete scene in their heads, similarly to a movie still, but the movie isn't actually playing in their heads, they go through these fabricated memories frame by frame. This is why they often react with overt hostility and threats (for example: legal action) towards those further probing into their accounts.

There are several possible reasons to be victim-playing that I can think of off the top of my head. I base these reasons in part on some of the cases I wrote about in this publication, some on other crime cases I have studied.

- If a person endured an earlier trauma, grew up in a household in which they were either abused or neglected, and they developed poor coping skills due to this, they may be prone to seek constant validation, going as far as craving public attention or sympathy and at times even monetary compensation for their plight.
Making up an outrageous story is a guaranteed way to do this and milk it indefinitely.

- If a person was attacked by someone but they choose to willfully implicate another (notorious) offender in the crime perpetrated on them, it may be due to them being aware that such stories do not sell without a "big name" attached to it. This could count for some of those who market their story in memoirs, on television programs or on blogs specifically designed for this purpose.

- If a person originally only misremembered that they were attacked by a notorious criminal (*False Memory Syndrome*), but they have already come forth with their story, they may fear or indeed face public ridicule and harassment, online as well as in person, if they later admit to having been wrong. They may be afraid to lose credibility, their social standing or the public support they may have grown accustomed to if they correct their error.

- They may even face legal charges and be held accountable for any monetary losses a publishing house or producer may suffer as a result.

- If a person originally misremembered who perpetrated an attack on them, but later becomes aware of their mistake, they may still believe that it is the general message that is important, rather than the facts. This message may for instance entail to be aware of your surroundings, that terrible things can still happen to good people, that one can regain their emotional and mental equilibrium after a crime, etc. pp.

- Due to another past trauma and/or mental health challenges, such as a personality disorder, someone may also develop unconventional fantasies, at times sexual in nature, that are conventionally frowned upon and/or clash with their or their community's religious views:
  In those cases it could happen that someone concocts a "murder fetish fiction" or BDSM edge-play story, but, upon feeling ashamed of their unconventional sexual fantasies, they relieve themselves of guilt or "responsibility" by turning themselves into a victim in these stories.
  In fact, they would either have to start believing these stories or make others believe that they were actual victims in order to cope with their feelings of shame and guilt.
  Ironically, the public outcry at what they endured both soothes their shame as well as reinforces it.

- There may also be people who, due to their religiosity, felt so terrible about having willfully engaged in a premarital sexual encounter that they must mentally transform the event into a rape scenario because they feel this is the only thing that may restore their virginity, at least emotionally and mentally.

- In some cases, an initially voluntary sexual encounter may have turned violent, and the – displaced and incorrect – impression that they were responsible or to blame for it may set certain thought processes in motion to help them cope.

- Some, though few, rape survivors engage in hypersexuality to "take back control" over their own bodies, their emotions and their lives.
  This isn't something that needs to physically occur, but would be possible to achieve via creating alternate storylines in their heads, mixing fantasy with reality, hence implicating a notorious offender or embellishing their story quite heavily.

- For those who display erratic, dramatic and overemotional behaviors which may be found in those who either experience a cluster B personality disorder or exhibit traits of one or more, one will rarely encounter mentions of fellow survivors of the same offender in their books, interviews, on their blogs or social media profiles, as this would mean having to compete for attention and sympathy with them.

- These may also be individuals who cannot bear the thought of being "just another survivor," just as they couldn't bear the thought of being just a random offender's victim, and so they may criticize or openly doubt other survivors. This lack of empathy is potentially dangerously damaging and traumatic for actual survivors.

- If they are active on social media, you may observe that certain individuals appear to have no identity outside of being/playing victims or survivors.
  Likewise, anything taking away attention from them is viewed as a hostile act, as competition.

- These people may have excessively studied the notorious offender's case, yet not necessarily well enough not to trip up when faced with surprise questions in interviews. They may then react hostilely and resort to accusations, threats and bouts of irrational (and misplaced) anger.

- They may repeat their fabricated survival story in the exact same manner, using the same vernacular while recounting elements of the story, giving the impression as if they memorized or rehearsed the story.

- Frame by frame analyses and interview stills may show micro-expressions of theirs that some experts believe to point to duping delight and deceptive mimic and gestures.

- If someone suffered the loss of a parental figure at a young age and had to fulfill the role of substitute parent for siblings or substitute partner for the remaining parent, their childhood needs may have been neglected. A consequence of this could lead to developing so-called "daddy fantasies" which do not have to be sexual in nature.

- They may split this über-father figure creation of theirs into different personas within their false rape narrative or domination/savior fantasy.
  Again, if the core fantasy revolves around unconventional sexuality, the creation of meeker father figures would help balance out this secret desire of being dominated and lessen their guilt.

Most importantly, we may not overlook the group of individuals whose mental health challenges are so much beyond their control that they cannot tell apart fantasy from reality anymore. Affected may be those with a *Delusional Disorder*, a cluster A personality disorder such as *Schizotypal*, those diagnosed with *Schizophrenia* or *Schizoaffective*, just to name a handful of feasible disorders responsible for such a break from reality.
I have examined a few such cases in the past, and they are easily enough identified by their *"word salad."* This metaphorical expression, also known as *paraphrasia* and disorganized speech, refers to the spoken or written practice of stringing words together which have no correlation to each other, resulting in apparently meaningless sentences. Clinicians also describe the phenomenon as coded language because the disorganized speaker

"holds the table to the code and only he can provide meanings to the otherwise incomprehensible dialect."
[Campbell's Psychiatric Dictionary by Robert Jean Campbell, 2009.]

A prominent example of someone producing word salad is the late cult leader Charles Manson.
It must be noted that not everyone producing *word salad* suffers from a psychiatric condition and I am naturally not suggesting that any unconfirmed Bundy survivor does.

However, it could just as well hold true that someone with such a disorder was indeed targeted by Bundy, yet cannot tell the events apart from what their neurodiverse minds added to the mix.

Some of my friends whom I discussed this with, were of the opinion that survivors fall into two categories, those whose story was true or untrue. It's not quite that easy, in my opinion. Having read through the previous chapters, we are left with:

Those of unsound mind whose memory was altered, and whose story is untrue due to *undeliberate* fabrication.

Those of sound mind whose memory was altered, and whose story is untrue due to *undeliberate* fabrications.

Those of unsound mind whose memory wasn't altered, and whose story is true.

Those of sound mind whose memory was altered, but whose story is still true.

Those of unsound mind whose memory was altered, but whose story is still true.

Those of sound mind whose memory wasn't altered, and who whose story is untrue due to *undeliberate* fabrications.

Those of unsound mind whose memory wasn't altered, and whose story is untrue due to **deliberate** fabrication.

Those of sound mind whose memory wasn't altered, and whose story is untrue due to **deliberate** fabrications.

And if one were so inclined, one could certainly add more possibilities to the mix.

Liz Arakelian's Self-Debunked Story

I was utterly intrigued when first stumbling upon Liz Arakelian's October 1, 2019 article *"I Believed I'd Encountered Ted Bundy – Until My Research Proved Me Wrong"* which she had written for the Medium.Com website.

Arakelian lived in Vail/Colorado at the time of one Julie Cunningham's disappearance. Almost fifteen years later, footage of Ted Bundy's impending execution was shown on TV, and Arakelian believed that she'd met the man years earlier while she was trying to hitch a ride. The man, she writes, made her blood run cold as soon as he opened his car door. The fact he had an axe in the backseat may have contributed to this feeling of unease. Arakelian continues,

"He didn't seem like the lumberjack type. He wasn't dressed for a foray into the woods to cut his own Christmas tree, either. It didn't add up, and for once in my young life, I made a smart decision."

She declined the ride.

Intending to write about how she eluded certain death that day in Vail, she discovered that several elements of her encounter didn't match, Bundy's M.O. and most significantly the timeline. At the time of her encounter Bundy was already on death row. Now, some might insist that if that was the case she had no other way to go than to admit she was wrong about running into Bundy. You'd be surprised as to the accounts I've heard and read over the years. There are enough women who insist that Bundy regularly escaped from death row in order to kill, and simply snuck back into prison afterwards. There is even one woman whose comments are strewn all over the internet, who insists that Bundy attempted to seduce and murder her in the visiting area at Raiford Prison. Arakelian could have followed suit, or she could have easily falsified the timeline of the encounter to present Bundy as a viable suspect. This level of honesty as it pertains to admitting the mistakenness of a Bundy encounter is as refreshing as it is rare.

Instead, Arakelian does what Mitzi Bader Erb & Co. could have done, which is to admit that they were in the same place as Bundy had been at one point in their lives, yet had had no dramatic encounter to share. Only the realization that being mindful of one's surroundings, listening to that small but persistent inner voice, can save lives. Arakelian admits that there are many possible explanations as to why the man had an axe in the backseat. But that isn't the point. The point is that it's indeed not necessary to fabricate or embellish an encounter in order to effectively appeal to the masses to take the necessary measures – including ignoring the social norm to act "nicely" – in order to stay out of harm's way.

Arakelian closes with,

*"I've now learned how important it is to **always** do your homework and research thoroughly before you publish something that could never have happened the way you'd long assumed it had."*

Our Malleable Memory: Dr. Elizabeth Loftus' Work

You may have heard someone state that "truth is perception" before. Elizabeth Loftus, professor of law and psychology at the University Of California in Irvine has proven how true this statement is.

In a 1974 study which she conducted together with John C. Palmer, she set out to prove how leading questions used during eyewitness interviews can influence, and alter, memory. The forty-five students participating in this laboratory experiment were each shown short clips of an automobile collision. Afterwards, Loftus and Palmer asked the "eyewitnesses" to describe the collision. The more emotionally laden words Loftus and Palmer used in their questions (hit, smashed) the more dramatic the events were later presented by participants. This was opposed to the group whose questions entailed neutral words such as "contacted," "connected," and "collided." Furthermore, the interviewers' language also influenced the estimated speed given by participants. Those who had been asked how fast the cars were going before they "smashed" into each other all "remembered" the car going at far greater speed than they actually had.

A week later the participants were brought back into the lab to answer more questions about what they remembered. Those whose memory had already been altered by emotional buzzwords, recalled seeing broken glass at the scene. – There had been no broken glass.

In the course of another experiment, Loftus was able to implant several otherwise mentally healthy individuals with the – false – memory of having gotten lost at the mall during infancy. The participants recalled the confusion, terror and kept adding details to the story, comparing the details in question with other, similar, emotions they had experienced on another occasion.

This, and in fact all of Loftus' work, demonstrates something I mentioned earlier in this publication. Human memory is not only malleable but we have a tendency to fill in memory gaps with details from similar events, or if there is no comparable event in our past, we combine it with fabricated scenarios of what appears most likely to us.

As it pertains to the unconfirmed Bundy survivor stories, we may think back to the missing door handle myth. This myth – although it has been repeatedly debunked by the best and brightest Bundy researchers – persists. There are few people, and even fewer Americans, who have not heard of Ted Bundy, the broken door handle, and the women he killed: "All" dark-haired with their hair parted in the middle, exactly the way his girlfriend Diane Edwards wore it. In reality, there is not one single photo of Diane Edwards on which she wears her hair parted down the middle. The only photo of this nature was provided by Joe Berlinger for his *"Conversations With A Killer: The Ted Bundy Tapes"* documentary for *Netflix*, and he accidentally picked the photo of the wrong woman, which I have written about on *CrimePiper*.

Most importantly, Bundy dated Edwards in the mid-/late 60's where this hairdo was not yet in style. But because True Crime writer Ann Rule wrote in her eternal bestseller *"The Stranger Beside Me"* that all of Bundy's victims looked like Edwards – indeed they "all looked like twins!" – our collective memory was altered to the point where 90% of Bundy students agree with Rule. This, although they have all seen both black and white, as well as color photos of the victims, whose only similarity to each other is that they're female, Caucasian and within the range of a healthy BMI.

And although Carol DaRonch was attacked by Bundy, Loftus – witness for the defense – proved that even DaRonch's memory had been partially altered.

While giving her statement at the Murray/Utah Police Station on November 8, 1974, the young woman relayed to police that her attacker had posed as a law enforcement officer. He had produced a badge to get her to accompany him to his car out in the Fashion Place Mall parking lot. When the officer asked DaRonch to describe the badge, he had held up his own badge for comparison, inquiring if it had looked anything like his. DaRonch confirmed this, and while on the stand during the trial that ensued in early 1976, she described "Bundy's" badge in great detail. Of course, it wasn't Bundy's fake badge she had described but the Murray police officer's.

This is how easily even actual victims are led and inadvertently manipulated in interviews.

Is it then difficult to believe that some of those women who truly do believe that Bundy was the one who kidnapped them, and who did not immediately after their abduction-experience contact police to have their statement taken, began misremembering certain details over time? That they, who often read about Bundy in great detail over the last four and a half decades, also filled in memory gaps with information they had read in Bundy literature or that their minds fabricated in order to make sense of the encounter?

I will close with yet another of Rhonda Stapley's quotes from her memoir. She writes that Bundy had been interviewed multiple times on death row, and that she had watched these interviews in question.

"There is one moment from those interviews, that I will never forget [...] The interviewer asked, "Ted, why did you kill?" With a sly smile, Ted shrugged his shoulders and raised an eyebrow. "Because I liked it.""

The only death row interview that had been recorded with a camera, and which was provided to the public, is Ted Bundy's final interview with Christian Reverend James Dobson, founder and owner of the *Focus On The Family* organization. It took place on January 23, 1989, a day prior to Bundy's execution. No such words were uttered by him in the interview.

In fact, the tidbit about Bundy's admission to having killed for hedonistic reasons stems from a conversation with FBI agent Bill Hagmaier. This conversation was never recorded on camera.

Sources & Further Reading

Publications:

<u>Ted Bundy</u>

The Bundy Murders: A comprehensive History by **Kevin M. Sullivan**, publisher: McFarland & Company, 2nd edition 2020, ISBN: 9781476681009.

The Trail of Ted Bundy: Digging up the untold Stories by **Kevin M. Sullivan**, publisher: WildBlue Press, 1st edition 2016, ISBN: 9781942266372.

The Bundy Secrets: Hidden Files on America's worst Serial Killer by **Kevin M. Sullivan**, publisher: WildBlue Press, 1st edition 2017, ISBN: 9781942266853.

Ted Bundy's Murderous Mysteries: The Many Victims of America's Most Infamous Serial Killer by **Kevin M. Sullivan**, publisher: WildBlue Press, 1st edition 2019, ISBN: 9781948239158.

The Encyclopedia of the Ted Bundy Murders by **Kevin Sullivan,** publisher: WildBlue Press, 1st edition 2020, ISBN: 9781948239615.

The Enigma Of Ted Bundy: The Questions And Controversies Surrounding America's Most Infamous Serial Killer by **Kevin Sullivan**, publisher: WildBlue Press, 1st edition 2020, ISBN: 9781952225383.

The Phantom Prince: My Life with Ted Bundy by **Elizabeth Kendall**, publisher: Madrona, 1st edition 1981, ISBN: 9780914842705; 2nd edition 2020, publisher: Abrams Books/Harry N. Abrams.

Ted Bundy: Conversations with a Killer by **Stephen Michaud** and **Hugh Aynesworth**, publisher: Signet, 2nd edition 1990, ISBN: 9780451163554.

The Only Living Witness by **Stephen Michaud** and Hugh **Aynesworth**, publisher: Authorlink, revised edition 1999, ISBN: 9781928704119.

Ted Bundy: A Visual Timeline by **Robert A. Dielenberg**, et al, publisher: Motion Mensura, ISBN: 9780994579218.

The Riverman: Ted Bundy And I Hunt For The Green River Killer by **Robert D. Keppel**, publisher: Pocket, revised edition 2004, ISBN: 9780743463959.

Terrible Secrets by **Robert D. Keppel** and **Stephen Michaud**, publisher: MT7 Film & E-Book Publishing, 1st edition 2012, ISBN: 9780985552022.

Ted Bundy, Celebrity Slayer by **George R. Dekle**, Kindle, 1st edition 2014, ASIN: B00LZD5QR8.

The Last Murder by **George R. Dekle**, publisher: Praeger, 1st edition 2011, ISBN: 9780313397431.

Ted & Ann: The Mystery Of A Missing Child And Her Neighbor Ted Bundy by **Rebecca Morris**, publisher: Createspace Independent Publishing Platform, 2nd edition 2013, ISBN: 9781484925089.

Ted Bundy: The Killer next Door by **Steven Winn**, publisher: Bantam, 1st edition 1979, ISBN: 9780553136371.

Ted Bundy: America's Most Evil Serial Killer by **Al Cimino**, publisher: Arcturus, 1st edition 2019, ISBN: 9781789505566.

Defending the Devil: My Story As Ted Bundy's Last Lawyer by **Polly Nelson**, publisher: William Morrow & Co., 1st edition 1980, ISBN: 9780688108236, 2nd edition 2018, ISBN: 9781635617757.

Reflections of Green River by **Sara: A Survivor**, publisher: Grass Butterfly Books, 1st edition 2016, ISBN: 9780974851051.

In Defense of Denial by **Sara: A Survivor**, publisher: Survivor Press, 1st edition 2016, ISBN: 9780974851044.

The Devil's Defender by **John Henry Browne**, publisher: Chicago Review, 1st edition 2018, ISBN: 9780912777672.

The Stranger Beside Me by **Ann Rule**, publisher: Planet Ann Rule, revised edition 2012, Kindle ASIN: B00AF09JS4.

I Survived Ted Bundy: The Attack, Escape And PTSD That Changed My Life by **Rhonda Stapley**, publisher: Galaxy-44, 1st edition 2016, ISBN: 9780997559309.

Reconstructing Sara: The lost Victim of Ted Bundy by **Sara A. Survivor**, publisher: Grass Butterfly Books, 1st edition 2016, ISBN: 9780974851037.

Conquering The Haunting Memories of Ted Bundy by **Victoria L.H.**, publisher: America Star Books, 1st edition 2011, ISBN: 9781462621224.

The Fight Of My Life by **Barbara Webb**, publisher: Christian Faith, Inc., 1st edition 2019, ISBN: 978-1643495811.

Ted Bundy: The Crimes Of America's Most Notorious Serial Killer by **Tom King**, Kindle, 1st edition 2017, ASIN: B071HXD1R7.

Serial Killers: Exploring The Horrific Crimes Of Jack The Ripper And Ted Bundy by **Tom King**, Kindle, 1st edition 2017, ASIN: B071K8QSDF.

Victims Of Ted Bundy: Washington State And Oregon by **Caitlin Elizabeth Thomson**, publisher: Jeanne Duval Editions, 1st edition 2011, ISBN: 9781621541608.

Serial Killers: The Psychosocial Development Of Humanity's Worst Offenders by **William Harmening**, publisher: Charles C. Thomas Pub. LTD, 1st edition 2014, ISBN: 9780398087883.

Masks Of A Lady Killer: Ted Bundy: College Girl's Horror! **[I'm not responsible for the placement of the apostrophe, E.B.]**, by "Dr." **Paul Dawson**, publisher: CreateSpace Independent Publishing Platform, 2012 edition ISBN: 9781505679755.

What Ted Did: The Story Of America's Most Prolific Serial Killer by **Frances J. Armstrong**, Kindle, ASIN: B06XK94961.

Ted Bundy: Killer Charm (Crime Shorts #2) by **David White**, Kindle, 1st edition 2015, ASIN: B013XHSLNO.

Ted Bundy: The College Girl Killer (True Crimes #9) by **Andrew Alexander**, Kindle, 1st edition 2016, ASIN: B01DFY0AGQ.

Serial Killers: Ted Bundy The Charismatic One (Serial Killer, Murder, Murderers, True Crime, Horror, Gore Book #2) by **Alex Allen**, Kindle, 1st edition 2016, ASIN: B01LFDKTME.

Chameleon: The True Story Of Ted Bundy by **Brian Lee Tucker**, Kindle, 1st edition 2014, ASIN: B00QR1BEHY.

The Case of Theodore (Ted) Bundy by **Steven G. Carley**, Kindle, 1st edition 2013, ASIN: B00EFYDBMQ.

Ted Bundy by **Laura Dobson**, Kindle, 1st edition 2016, ASIN: B01CW1AV8K.
Ted Bundy by **George Stietz**, Kindle, 1st edition 2013, ASIN: B00EKWU3EW.

Serial Killers: Profiles Of Today's Most Terrifying Criminals, (>Bundy chapter/mentions) publisher: TIME LIFE Books, 1st edition 1992, ISBN: 9780783500003.

Ted Bundy: Unmasked (Serial Series Book #1) by **Michael Vincent**, Kindle, 1st edition 2017, ASIN: B0776MYPW2.

Summary And Analysis Of The Stranger Beside Me: The Shocking Inside Story Of Serial Killer Ted Bundy: Based On The Book By Ann Rule, publisher: Worth Books, 1st edition 2017, ASIN: B06VSQN6HT.

Murder Tales: Ted Bundy by **H.N. Lloyd**, Kindle, 1st edition 2016, ASIN: B01C1Y46YI.

Bundy: Portrait Of A Serial Killer by **Robert Keller**, publisher: CreateSpace Independent Publishing Platform, 1st edition 2017, ISBN: 9781548730673.

"I'm Not Guilty!": The Case Of Ted Bundy (Development Of The Violent Mind, Book #1) by **Dr. Al Carlisle**, publisher: Carlisle Legacy Books LLC, revised edition 2020, ISBN: 9781952043000.

The 1976 Psychological Assessment Of Ted Bundy (Development Of The Violent Mind Series) by **Dr. Al Carlisle**, publisher: Carlisle Legacy Books LLC, revised edition 2020, ISBN: 9781952043093.

Bundy: The Deliberate Stranger by **Richard W. Larsen**, Kindle, 1st edition 1980, ASIN: B01FJ0T5EW.

The Secret Psychic Files: The Men Who Caught Ted Bundy by **David Yasmer**, publisher: CreateSpace Independent Publisher, 1st edition 2017, ISBN: 978-1547109401.

Inside The Mind Of America's Most Glorified Serial Killer: Ted Bundy by **Kathy Lee**, publisher: CreateSpace Independent Publishing Platform, 1st edition 2016, ISBN: 978-1537524696.

Mysteries Of The Criminal Mind by **TIME LIFE Editors**, (>Bundy chapters/mentions) 1st edition 2015, ISBN: 978-1618933539.

The Professional Serial Killer And The Career Of Ted Bundy by **Bonnie M. Rippo**, publisher: X, 1st edition 2007, ISBN: 9780595423842.

Psychology

Prison Groupies: The Shocking True Story Of Women Who Love America's Deadliest Criminals by **Clifford L. Linedecker**, publisher: Pinnacle Books, 1st edition 1993, ISBN: 9781558177024.

Women Who Love Men Who Kill by **Sheila Isenberg**, publisher: Backinprint, 2nd edition 2000, ISBN: 9780595003990.

Michelle Remembers by **Michelle Smith** and **Dr. Lawrence Pazdar**, publisher: Congdon Lattes, 1st edition 1980, ISBN: 978-0865530010.

Sybil Exposed: The Extraordinary Story Behind The Famous Multiple Personality Disorder Case by **Debbie Newman**, publisher: Free Press, 1st edition 2011, ISBN: 9781439168271.

Forensic Aspects Of Dissociative Identity Disorder by Karnac Books (publisher), 1st edition 2008, ISBN: 9781855755963.

Guilty By Reason Of Insanity by **Dr. Dorothy Otnow Lewis**, M.D., publisher: Ivy Books, 1st edition 1998, ISBN: 9780804118873.

Without A Conscience: The Disturbing World Of Psychopaths Among Us by **Dr. Robert D. Hare**, publisher: The Guilford Press, 1st edition 1999, ISBN: 9781572304512.

The Sociopath Next Door by **Dr. Martha Stout**, publisher: Harmony, 1st edition 2006, ISBN: 9780767915823.

Dangerous Personalities: An FBI Profiler Shows You How To Protect Yourself From Harmful People by **Joe Navarro** (ann.: former Bundy investigator from Utah), publisher: Rodale, reprint edition 2018, ISBN: 9781635653366.

Emotional Blackmail by **Dr. Susan Forward**, publisher: Harper Collins, 1998 edition, ISBN: 9780060928971.

The Mask Of Sanity: An Attempt To Clarify Some Issues About The So-Called Psychopathic Personality by **Hervey M. Cleckley**, publisher: Echo Point Books & Media, 1st edition 1941/2015 edition ISBN: 9781626549661.

Why Do I Do That?: Psychological Defense Mechanisms And The Hidden Way They Shape Our Lives by **Joseph Burgo, M.D.,** publisher: New Rise Press, 2012 edition, ISBN: 9780988443129.

Omgiven Av Psykopater: Så Undviker Du Bli Uttnyttjad Av Andra by **Thomas Erikson**, publisher: Forum, 1st edition 2017, ISBN: 9789175039510.

Ärlig Och Snäll: En Viktig Bok Om Kvinnliga Psykopater by **Håkan Olofsson**, publisher: Vulkan, 1st edition 2019, ISBN: 9789163994395.

Sadisten by **Lydia Benecke**, publisher: Ehrenwirth, 1st edition 2015, ISBN: 9783431038996.

Psychopathinnen by **Lydia Benecke**, publisher: Ehrenwirth, 1st edition 2018, ISBN: 9783431039962.

Confessions Of A Sociopath: A Life Spent Hiding In Plain Sight by **M.E. Melodie**, publisher: Crown, reprint edition 2014, ISBN: 978-0307956651.

Stop Caretaking The Borderline Or Narcissist by **Margalis Fjelstad**, publisher: Rl, 2014 edition, ISBN: 9781442238329.

Stop Walking On Eggshells by **Randi Kreger** and **Paul T.T. Mason MS**, publisher: New Harbinger, 2010 edition, ISBN: 9781572246904.

The Bipolar Disorder Survival Guide: What You And Your Family Need To Know by **David J. Miklowitz**, publisher: The Guilford Press, 1st edition 2002, ISBN: 9781572305250.

Welcome To The Jungle: Everything You Ever Wanted To Know About Bipolar But Were Too Freaked Out To Ask by Hilary T. Smith, publisher: Conari Press, 1st edition 2010, ISBN: 9781573244725.

Misdiagnosis And Dual Diagnosis Of Gifted Children And Adults: ADHD, Bipolar, OCD, Asperger's, Depression And Other Disorders by **James T. Webb, Nadia E. Webb and Edward R. Amend**, publisher: Great Potential Press, 1st edition 2004, ISBN: 9780910707640.

The Myth Of Repressed Memory by **Dr. Elizabeth Loftus**, publisher: Griffin, 1996 edition, ISBN: 9780312141233.

Witness For The Defense: The Accused, The Eyewitness And The Expert Who Puts Memory On Trial by **Elizabeth Loftus**, publisher: St. Martin's Griffin, 1992 edition, ISBN: 9780312084554.

The Memory Illusion: Remembering, Forgetting And The Science Of False Memory by **Dr. Julia Shaw**, publisher: Random House, 2017 edition, ISBN: 9781847947611.

Perv: The Sexual Deviant In All Of Us by **Jesse Bering**, publisher: Scientific American / Farrer, Straus, Giroux / reprint edition 2014, ISBN: 9780374534837.

Predators: Pedophiles, Rapists And Other Sex Offenders by Dr. Anna C. Salter, publisher: Basic Books, 1st edition 2004, ISBN: 9780465071739.

The Pleasure's All Mine: A History Of Perverse Sex by **Julie Peakman**, publisher: Reaktion, 2013 edition, ISBN: 978-1780231853.

Sex & Punishment: Four Thousand Years Of Judging Desire by **Eric Berkowitz**, publisher: Counterpoint, 2013 edition, ISBN: 9781619021556.

Abnormal Psychology by **Robin Rosenberg** and **David Kossner**, publisher: Worth, 2nd edition 2009, ISBN: 978-0716717287.

Introduction To Forensic Psychology by **Curtis R. Bartol** and **Anne M. Bartol**, publisher: Sage, 5th edition 2018, ISBN: 9781506387246.

Klinisk Forensisk Psykologi by **Åsa Eriksson** and **Knut Sturidsson**, publisher: Studentlitteratur AB, 1st edition 2017, ISBN: 9789144114491.

DSM-5 (Diagnostics And Statistics Manual Of Mental Disorders), publisher: American Psychiatric Publishing, 5th edition 2013, ISBN: 9780890425558.

Criminology

Serial Murder by **Ronald M. Holmes**, publisher: Sage, 2nd edition 1998, ISBN: 9780761913665.

Serial Offenders: Current Thoughts, Recent Findings by **Louis B. Schlesinger**, publisher: CRC Press, 1st edition 2000, ISBN: 9780849322365.

Crime Classification Manual, publisher: Wiley, 3rd edition 2013, ISBN: 978-1118305058.

Whoever Fights Monsters by **Robert K. Ressler**, publisher: St. Martin's Press, 2nd edition 1998, ISBN: 978-0312950446.

Neuroscience & -psychology

Neuroscience: Exploring The Brain by **Conners**, **Bear**, **Paradiso** et al, publisher: Lippincott Williams and Wilkins, 3rd edition 2006, ISBN: 978-0781760034

A Mind To Crime: The Controversial Link Between The Mind And Criminal Behavior by **Ann Moir** and **David Jessel**, publisher: Penguin, 1st edition 1995, ISBN: 9780451196293.

The Brain by **Dr. David Eagleman**, publisher: Vintage, ill. 2017 edition, ISBN: 9780525433446.

The Murderer Next Door: Why The Brain Is Designed To Kill by **David M. Buss**, publisher: Penguin, reprint edition 2006, ISBN: 978-0143037057.

The Psychopath Inside: A Neuroscientist's Personal Journey Into The Dark Side Of The Brain by **James Fallon**, publisher: Portfolio, 2014 edition, ISBN: 9781617230158.

Various

Among The Lowest Of The Dead: The Culture Of Capital Punishment (Law, Meaning And Violence) by **David Von Drehle**, publisher: University Of Michigan Press, 2006 edition, ISBN: 9780472031238.

Games Criminals Play: How You Can Profit By Knowing Them by **Bud Allen** and **Diane Bosta**, publisher: Rae John Pub Co., 1st edition 1981, ISBN: 9780960522606.

The Joy Of Sex by **Alex Comfort**, publisher: Quartet, 1st edition 1974, ISBN: 9780671216498.

Files:

https://crimepiperblog.wordpress.com/files-section/
(All sources listed on blog)

Blogs:

CrimePiper
www.crimepiperblog.wordpress.com

Reconstructing Sara by "Sara A. Survivor"
https://reconstructingsara.com

Ted Bundy Research and Musings by Cynthia Walker
https://tbundymusings.blogspot.com

What's Left After by Meg S.
www.whatisleftafter.wordpress.com

Wild Blue Press/Kevin M. Sullivan
https://wildbluepress.com/true-crime-author-kevin-m-sullivan/

Confessions Of A Bundyphile by E.J. Hammon
www.confessionsofabundyphile.com

Websites & Articles:

King County Archives (KCA)
www.kingcounty.gov and www.archivesearch.kingcounty.gov

Wikipedia articles on Ted Bundy, Utah, Washington, California, Idaho, Florida, Santa Rosa Hitchhiker Murders, Julia "Julie" Cunningham…
Link:
www.wikipedia.org/en

Murderpedia articles on Ted Bundy, Santa Rosa Hitchhiker Murders.
www.murderpedia.com

Santa Rosa Hitchhiker Murders
www.santarosahitchhikermurders.com

Utah State Parks & Recreation
https://stateparks.utah.gov/ and https://www.facebook.com/utahstateparks/

"*How To Survive A Fast River Current*" by **Diana Gerstacker**, June 10, 2014 for **The Active Times**.
Link:

https://www.theactivetimes.com/how-survive-fast-river-current

The National Center for Biotechnology Information
Links:
https://www.ncbi.nlm.nih.gov/pmc/articles/PMC5960855/
and
https://www.ncbi.nlm.nih.gov/pmc/articles/PMC4650306/

Auto/Truck/Fleet – Paint Cross Reference, aka "PaintRef"
https://paintref.com/paintref/index.shtml

"Did The Rosary Stop A Ted Bundy From Killing A College Student?" by **Alex R. Hey**, May 16, 2017 for **Epic Pew**.
Link:
https://epicpew.com/rosary-stop-serial-killers-rampage/

"How I Knew The Priest Who Ministered To Ted Bundy & His Victims" by **Domenico Bettinelli**, May 14, 2009 for **BettNet**.
Link:
https://www.bettnet.com/how_i_knew_the_priest_who_ministered_to_ted_bundy_his_vi
ctims/

"3 Close Calls With Ted Bundy" by **Susanne Crawford**, July 5, 2015 for **Spectrum**.
https://eu.thespectrum.com/story/life/2015/07/05/close-calls-utah-ted-bundy/29742385/

"Real 'Sybil' Admits Multiple Personalities Were Fake" by **Lynn Neary**, October 20, 2011 for **NPR**.
Link:
https://www.npr.org/2011/10/20/141514464/real-sybil-admits-multiple-personalities-were-fake

"The Myth Of Multiple Personality Disorder" by **Esther Inglis-Arkell**, December 7, 2011, for **Gizmodo**.
Link:
https://io9.gizmodo.com/the-myth-of-multiple-personality-disorder-5865263

"Sybil Exposed: A Look At Dissociative Identity Disorder" by **Andrew Nanton, M.D.**, May 2, 2012, for **Psychiatric Times**.
Link:
https://www.psychiatrictimes.com/view/sybil-exposed-look-dissociative-identity-disorder

"Boys Reach Sexual Maturity Younger And Younger" by **Joshua Goldstein**/Max-Planck-Gesellschaft, August 8, 2011 for **AlphaGalileo**.
Link:
https://www.alphagalileo.org/en-gb/Item-Display/ItemId/79509?returnurl=https://www.alphagalileo.org/en-gb/Item-Display/ItemId/79509

"Man's Obsessions Turn Deadly" by **Dennis B. Roddy** and **Jim McKinnon**, January 30, 1998 for the **Pittsburgh-Post Gazette**.
Link:
https://www.newspapers.com/clip/35616196/janla-carr-kills-self-father-bundy-p2/

"Suicide Comes Year After Daughter's Death" by **Laure Cioffi**, January 30, 1998 for **North Hills News Records**.
Link:
https://www.newspapers.com/clip/35653097/janla-carr-article-2/

FBI information on CODIS
https://www.fbi.gov/services/laboratory/biometric-analysis/codis

FBI file of Ted Bundy
https://vault.fbi.gov/Ted%20Bundy%20

YouTube: Mary Conely's channel
https://www.youtube.com/channel/UCyJpiNEoBpiRYqODsE5gfFg

"Penn State Professor Recalls Close Encounters With Bundy" by Samantha York on March 7, 2019 for WJAC6
Link:

https://wjactv.com/news/local/penn-state-professor-recalls-close-encounters-with-ted-bundy

Photos:
Ted Bundy's "Utah Kill Kit," taken by Detective Jerry Thompson, 1975, courtesy of SLCSO and KCA
Dan Kritsonis comment on CrimePiper, 2019
Janla Carr 1988 passport photo, courtesy of the Pittsburgh-Post Gazette
Mary Conely 1971, My Heritage website
Mary Conely 1972, My Heritage website
Google Maps Jacksonville, Florida, 2020
Pensacola Files excerpt
Underage victim collage, single images via KCA, Pocatello Police, FL State Archive, public domain.
Facebook comment by (*name redacted) from Ted Bundy: UNLIMITED (now defunct), 2019
Facebook post by R. Worth* from 2019
Photos from YouTube video comment section 2019
Photo of William Lloyd Marshall from Aurore Sage's now defunct tumblr page
Kevin M. Sullivan's copy of 1975 Sylvia Valint's (now: Meixner) follow-up report by Roger Dunn

About The Author

Erin Banks is a Northern German-born Specialist In Media & Information Sciences, Simultaneous Interpreter, Autism Advocate and writer with Scandinavian and American roots who currently resides in the UK. She used to own the *CrimePiper* Wordpress blog and still helps manage it.

She has contributed chapters to French author Anne Cossé's book, *"Could YOU Be Autistic? How One Realizes They Are On The Spectrum,"* and Kevin M. Sullivan's sixth book on the Ted Bundy case, *"The Enigma Of Ted Bundy: The Controversies And Questions Surrounding America's Most Infamous Serial Killer."*

"Ted Bundy: Examining The Unconfirmed Survivor Stories" is her first Kindle publication. Her next book, a work of fiction, is loosely scheduled to appear in 2022.

Printed in Great Britain
by Amazon

63469379R00088